THE OFFICIAL
itv SPORT GUIDE

FORMULA ONE
GRAND PRIX >>>>> 2002

THIS IS A CARLTON BOOK
This edition published in 2002 for Index Books Ltd
10 9 8 7 6 5 4 3 2 1

Text and design copyright © Carlton Books Limited 2002

A CIP catalogue record for this book is available from the British Library

The publisher has taken reasonable steps to check the accuracy of the facts
contained herein at the time of going to press but can take no responsibility
for any errors

ISBN 1 84222 557 X

Project Editor: Kerrin Edwards
Project Art Direction: Mark Lloyd
Cover Design by: Steve Lynn
Design by: Phil Gambrill
Production: Lisa French
Picture Research: Debora Fioravanti

Printed in Italy

THE OFFICIAL
itv SPORT GUIDE

FORMULA ONE
GRAND PRIX >>>>> 2002

Bruce Jones

INDEX

CONTENTS

FOREWORD BY MARTIN BRUNDLE 6

Chapter 1

Analysis of the 2002 GP Season 8

Ferrari Team News 10

Michael Schumacher 14

Rubens Barrichello 15

BAR Team News 36

Jacques Villeneuve 38

Olivier Panis 39

Renault Sport (formerly Benetton) Team News 40

Jarno Trulli 42

Jenson Button 43

McLaren Team News 16

David Coulthard 20

Kimi Räikkönen 21

Williams Team News 22

Ralf Schumacher 26

Juan Pablo Montoya 27

Sauber Team News 28

Nick Heidfeld 30

Felipe Massa 31

Jordan Team News 32

Giancarlo Fisichella 34

Takuma Sato 35

Jaguar Racing Team News 44

Eddie Irvine 46

Pedro de la Rosa 47

Prost Team News 48

Jos Verstappen 49

Prost No. 2 driver 49

Arrows Team News 50

Heinz-Harald Frentzen 51

Enrique Bernoldi 51

Minardi Team News 52

Alex Yoong 53

Minardi No. 2 driver 53

Toyota Team News 54

Mika Salo 55

Allan McNish 55

Chapter 2

Toyota: F1's Newest Team 56

Technical Insight 60

Setting-up a Car for Different GP Circuits 64

Technical Glossary 67

Chapter 3

Review of 2001 68

The Year in Pictures 70

Australian GP 72

Malaysian GP 74

Canadian GP 86

European GP 88

French GP 90

British GP 92

German GP 94

Hungarian GP 96

Belgian GP 98

Italian GP 100

United States GP 102

Japanese GP 104

Final Tables 106

Chapter 4

Glamour on the Grid 108

Formula One Records 112

Brazilian GP 76

San Marino GP 78

Spanish GP 80

Austrian GP 82

Monaco GP 84

Chapter 5

Preview of the 2002 Venues 120

The 2002 Grand Prix Chart 126

Picture Acknowledgements 128

>> FOREWORD

I am looking forward to the 2002 Formula One season with great anticipation and excitement. We have been starved of Formula One activity because of the new, unusual and ultimately unsuccessful regulation of banning any track work in the final two months of last year.

Never has the testing activity been so intense therefore as in the early part of 2002, but will the hard work pay off? Can any of the teams catch Ferrari, let alone beat them? Will Michael Schumacher take his third successive and fifth overall title?

The reigning World Champions will undoubtedly improve their already dominant car. Such was their advantage last season there is even rumour that Ferrari will start the year with the 2001 car. I would be surprised if this happens and it would be a mistake. It is always better to develop the latest, ultimately faster, version and take the early reliability setbacks.

McLaren and Williams each have three difficult and crucial steps to make. Firstly close the deficit to Ferrari from last season. Secondly, match the Italian stallion's winter improvements. Thirdly, somehow create an advantage to make the wins possible. Not easy.

McLaren Mercedes-Benz lose the speed and experience of Hakkinen but gain the precocious talent of Kimi Räikkönen, who will be under relentless pressure to deliver. David Coulthard was at his career best last season. More of the same with better reliability will put him in World Championship contention. Can McLaren give him the car he needs? Has the Adrian Newey to Jaguar 'near miss' created instability? Will they quickly and effectively make good use of the move to Michelin tyres?

BMW Williams had a great package at the end of last season and, with further improvements and Michelin's season-long experience of grooved tyres, will definitely win more races. Montoya looks supremely confident in himself and his ability to fight Michael Schumacher wheel to wheel. Ralf Schumacher has to fight back or he will effectively be written off. He can do it.

Sauber had a fabulous 2001 but now without Räikkönen will they have improved the car enough to maintain that fourth place in the Constructors' Championship? Heidfeld has come of age though and looks capable of leading the team well. Benetton has 'morphed' into the works Renault team but are still based in the UK. Superfast but cautious racer Jarno Trulli joins new team mate - and my tip for the 'positive surprise of the year' - Jenson Button. Jenson has matured in every respect but he must rise above the pressure and speculation surrounding the security of his drive, especially with Fernando Alonso in the wings as official test driver.

Jordan have changed their technical organisation after a disappointing 2001 and need to deliver more podiums and points. If the car works well, the Honda engine should be well up to the job. Fisichella can be superfast but not every day. New boy Sato will be a revelation but ultimately a painful learning year must beckon. Jordan deserve to do well but this will depend on reliability. BAR Honda still seem to have senior personnel woes but new team principal David Richards' arrival should create some stability. How will Villeneuve react to the departure of manager and friend Craig Pollock? Can the team find speed at this crucial time? The ingredients are all there but not mixing well right now.

Jaguar have imported some management talent from the sister Ford Rally team. Niki Lauda still calls the shots but his previous boss Jacques Nasser has left the scene. Irvine is fast and committed but can't lead a team. De la Rosa is underrated but needs to toughen up in the head to deliver his full potential. I, personally, really want Jaguar to do well. Orange Arrows now have the same works engine as Jaguar and will surely improve. Minardi remain everybody's favourite underdog and technical regulation stability will undoubtedly help the back end of the grid in general. Let's hope Prost make it through the bankruptcy courts to Melbourne and beyond.

Finally, new boys Toyota. A bold gamble to 'do a Ferrari' and make both the chassis and engine. It will be painful from time to time but by mid-season they will be respectable.

We will all miss Murray Walker behind the F1 ITV microphone but James Allen and I, along with the rest of the team, will be working hard to keep you informed at all times.

Enjoy your motor racing and see you on the grid.

To keep track of all the latest developments for the 2002 Formula One Grand Prix Championship, go to ITV's own excellent website, itv.com/f1

ANALYSIS OF THE 2002 GRAND PRIX SEASON

So, is Ferrari going to stay on the top of the pile in the season ahead, or is the order of Formula One going to be shuffled by a return to the top for either Williams or McLaren? Or what chance is there of another team outstripping them all? That's the beauty of Formula One, as you never can tell what's going to happen.

With the rules and regulations remaining all but the same as last year, it would take a brave person to bet against Ferrari's Michael Schumacher racing to his fifth world title and thus pulling level in the all-time rankings with Juan Manuel Fangio, the driver who dominated the 1950s. Indeed, with support from the ever-improving Rubens Barrichello, Ferrari ought to be looking at another constructors' title too.

But that's ignoring the fact that Williams was every bit the equal of Ferrari at the end of 2001, although a question-mark remains over whether their drivers, Ralf Schumacher and Juan Pablo Montoya, will take points off each other's title bid. McLaren isn't a team that ever stays down for long – well, finishing second overall in both championships last year was 'down' by their standards. David Coulthard is joined by last year's hottest rookie Kimi Räikkönen, and Mercedes is sure to offer them a more competitive engine this time around, so watch out. Looking to harness every technical advantage available, McLaren could well have made a strong move by ditching Bridgestone tyres for rubber from Michelin, especially as many of the sport's insiders reckon that the French tyres will be even stronger in the company's second season back in Formula One.

If you want to look for a dark horse – a team that will surprise the pedigrees – then the newly-renamed Renault Sport team will be looking to build on the progress achieved late last year by Benetton when it was

Fast Forward: Williams is the team with the most to look forward to after a strong finish in the 2001 World Championship

running the company's revolutionary, wide-angle V10 engine. The opposition is certainly keeping an eye out for them.

The fact that the front runners were able to lap up to three seconds per lap faster in 2001 than they had the year before despite aerodynamic hobbling was thanks to the level of competition between the two tyre suppliers. Not surprisingly, this caused the sport's governing body to look at amending the rules in the interest of keeping speeds in check in the name of safety. However, a further reduction in downforce isn't thought advisable as it would make the cars unstable. Thoughts of reducing engine capacity can't be countenanced either, as the existing Concorde Agreement means that the engine rules can't be changed until the end of 2007.

Talking of safety, proof abounds that the cars are safer than ever, as shown by Prost driver Luciano Burti surviving a massive, near-head-on accident at Blanchimont during the Belgian GP that would almost certainly have killed him had it happened even just a few years before.

Some interesting new technology will also be used this year but, sadly, you won't be able to see it as it's not visible. The technology in question is pit-to-car telemetry, meaning that the engineers will be able to alter their cars' performance during the race by changing fuel maps or differential settings while the cars are on the move. And due to teams encoding their data, it's unlikely that any team could end up changing the settings on another team's cars.

Talk late last year of the teams facing a financial crisis was very realistic, with Prost put into liquidation in November, but potential buyers were circulating. The teams have also been talking to Kirch, leading shareholders of TV rights holders SLEC, about gaining a greater share of the TV revenue in future, and the leading manufacturers are talking of forming a breakaway series for 2007.

NB: Please note that not all the drivers had been confirmed at the time this book closed for press. Where not sure, this year I have rounded up the situation rather than take a calculated guess as I have done in the past. Furthermore, like last year when the future of Minardi was in the balance until the middle of January, Prost is heading into this winter on an unstable financial footing and so I hope that the French team has weathered the storm and will be ready to go racing in Melbourne.

FERRARI

TEAM AT THE TOP

Not so many years ago, it was hard to imagine Ferrari rediscovering its winning touch. Now, it's hard to imagine them losing it, and it would be a brave person to bet against the Italian team taking its fourth consecutive constructors' title.

Make no mistake about it: Ferrari will start this year's world championship in pole position for honours. Williams may have been snapping at its heels in 2001, with McLaren not far behind, but that will only spur on the world's most famous team to greater heights.

The change in the aerodynamic regulations for last year seemed to suit Ferrari, but their huge success in scoring nine wins from 17 starts owed as much to class-leading reliability and the considerable input of Michael Schumacher, who made it two drivers' titles on the trot. That Ferrari's tally was 77 points ahead of any other team was also down to second driver Rubens Barrichello, who is staying on, confident that he can win races in 2002. So, expect Ferrari to be competitive from start to finish. Technical director Ross Brawn summed this up by saying: "There's always huge expectation of Ferrari. Winning the drivers' title in 2000 took the monkey off our back, but the team is still extremely competitive and wants to win every race it enters."

Study the combination of an unlimited budget, one of the most powerful engines, superb in-house facilities including their own

test track, sharp management, a master tactician on the pitwall plus two top-notch drivers, and you can understand why Ferrari ought to succeed again. However, rival teams have even more to fear as Ferrari is said to be developing a revolutionary transmission that could, at a stroke, render all others inadequate.

The way in which it is alleged to differ is that instead of the engine transferring its power to the wheels via a clutch, Ferrari will do away with the clutch. You might consider this unnecessary since today's semi-automatic gearboxes make gearchanging a cinch, but by using its differentials to perform the function of a clutch instead, Ferrari's and Sachs' boffins have potentially reduced the amount of power that will be lost between the engine and the driven wheels. The weight saved by not having to carry a clutch will be useful, too. If this revolutionary transmission exists and it works, expect others to try to follow suit as soon as possible.

On the Ball: In his role as Ferrari's tactician, Ross Brawn can't afford to miss a trick

A winner from the off

The Ferrari F2001 was the pick of the pack. Described as being an evolution rather than a revolution, it continued a trend that Ferrari has been enjoying in the past four years since stability came to the team, with Rory Byrne leading the design team under Brawn's guidance. With teams forced to run a high-nose format, Ferrari was laughing as it had stuck with this route in the past when McLaren had hung their noses low. And the F2001's front end was the most effective of them all, affording its drivers the turn-in they desired. On top of this, the aerodynamic package appeared to offer the most downforce, something that was harnessed to good use in qualifying.

Michael set the alarm bells ringing when he won the opening race in Australia. He won again in Malaysia, but this was due more to inspired tyre choice after a downpour had cars aquaplaning, as Ferrari alone opted to send its cars back out on intermediate tyres. And how this paid off as Michael and Rubens stormed up the order then broke clear to take a one-two result as they pleased.

This storming form caused their rivals to panic – as Ferrari traditionally starts slowly then improves – but cracks appeared at the Brazilian GP. Michael may have started from pole, but he was outmuscled by Williams' rookie Juan Pablo Montoya then outraced by McLaren's David Coulthard. He later claimed that he was caught out by having the wrong settings for the wet. This was plausible, as was the fact that the team's San Marino GP was spoiled by opting for Bridgestone's harder rubber. Unusually for Ferrari, Michael's retirement was due to a mechanical failure, with part of his brake ducting damaging a wheel rim. However, blaming a poor third set of tyres for Michael's drop-off in pace in the Spanish GP was less believable. Some said that it was more likely that this was because he'd been told to slow down, as the team didn't want a repeat of the suspension failure that had led to Rubens' retirement in that same race. Actually, it was due to the tyres turning on their rims.

At this stage, Rubens' second year of being number two to Michael didn't look as though it was going to be a success as he appeared to be increasingly fragile mentally. This was never more plain than when he fell apart at his home race: Rubens qualified only sixth at Interlagos, then crashed his way out of the race, clashing with Ralf Schumacher for the second race in succession. However, with continuity having its benefits, contracts were renewed as early as the run-up to last year's Monaco GP. The powerbase of Michael, team chief Jean Todt, Brawn and engine guru Paolo Martinelli will all be staying at Ferrari until the end of 2004, with Rubens extending his deal to stay until the end of this year.

It also became clear that Michael was letting Montoya rile him, with his attempt to overtake around the outside in Austria both unnecessary and expensive as it dropped him to sixth. Only ordering Rubens to pull over and let him through to second on the final lap saved face. However, the ructions were huge, with many saying that Ferrari was bringing the sport into disrepute. More realistically, once Rubens had calmed down, he knew that he had a clause in his contract specifying that he must let Michael through when told to do so.

But still the wins kept coming. However, one factor that was making life harder for Ferrari than they would have wished was that their engine was thirstier than its rivals', offering McLaren's more-economical Mercedes an advantage when it came to deciding race tactics – something that was shown at the United States GP when

Mika Hakkinen's longer first stint helped him into a lead that he was to keep to the finish.

A clear sign of the progress that Ferrari made was the way in which it fought back from being thrashed by Williams on the straights of Hockenheim to take the battle to the same team the next time they raced on a similar track, at Monza. This gain was due to aerodynamic modifications and a more powerful engine. Yet it was also down to Bridgestone producing a tyre that was softer than the Michelins used by Williams, but which also lasted better.

Ferrari used to be a team of fluctuating fortunes, but Todt's reign has brought continuity, as shown by the fact that after years of constant improvement since Todt arrived, Ferrari was able to claim its third consecutive constructors' title. However, Todt never lets success turn his head, and he summed up why he never basks in the glory for long. "We're in a business where things change very quickly, so we must focus on the future," he said. So, what chance a fourth consecutive constructors' title in 2002?

Practice Makes Perfect: The highly professional Ferrari pit crew rehearse their pit stops whenever there's a spare moment over a Grand Prix weekend

One by building tiny cars with their engines at the back in the late 1950s. But it was saved by having the ideal engine when the regulations changed again in 1961 and Phil Hill stormed to the title. John Surtees was champion for Ferrari in 1964, but the former world motorcycle champion left when internal politics became too much for him. And the politics of blame and counter-blame kept success at bay until Niki Lauda combined with Luca di Montezemolo to drag the team from its darkest hours to win the title in 1975 and 1977. Jody Scheckter made it three drivers' titles in five years for Ferrari in 1979, but then Ferrari couldn't match the progress of British teams Williams, Brabham and McLaren and failed to guide a driver to the title until, finally, Michael Schumacher saved them in 2000.

The Top Tool: Michael Schumacher and Rubens Barrichello both enjoyed racing the best car/engine package of the 2001 season

FOR THE RECORD

Country of origin	Italy
Team base	Maranello, Italy
Website	www.ferrari.it
Active in Formula One	From 1950
Grands Prix contested	653
Wins	144
Pole positions	148
Fastest laps	147

DRIVERS + RESULTS 2001

Driver	Nationality	Races	Wins	Pts	Pos
Rubens Barrichello	Brazilian	17	-	56	3rd
Michael Schumacher	German	17	9	123	1st

CAR SPECIFICATIONS

Team principal	Jean Todt
Technical director	Ross Brawn
Team manager	Stefano Domenicali
Chief designer	Rory Byrne
Chief engineer	Luca Baldisserri
Test drivers	Luca Badoer & Luciano Burti
Chassis	Ferrari F2002
Engine	Ferrari V10
Tyres	Bridgestone

Formula One's constant

Ferrari has been part of the world championship since its inception in 1950, a record that no other team can claim. It wasn't a great success to begin with as Alfa Romeo swept all before it, but Ferrari's breakthrough came in 1951 at the British GP when chunky Argentinian José "Froilan" Gonzalez was the pick of the pack at Silverstone. And, since then, a further 143 wins have been collected by the red cars bearing the badge of the Prancing Horse, along with world titles for 10 of its drivers and 11 victories in the constructors' championship, which has run alongside the drivers' championship every year since 1958.

Ferrari's Formula One history has been annoyingly fitful for its millions of fans, the *tifosi*. Alberto Ascari cleaned up when the regulations changed in 1952 and repeated the feat the following year. Then Juan Manuel Fangio was champion for Ferrari in 1956. Britain's Mike Hawthorn followed suit two years later. However, Ferrari was slow to react to British teams revolutionising Formula

MICHAEL SCHUMACHER

AIMING FOR THREE IN A ROW

The most successful driver in Formula One history has few records left to aim at, but becoming only the second driver to win three titles in a row is his target.

TRACK NOTES

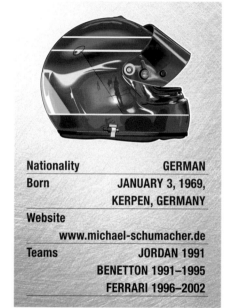

Nationality	GERMAN
Born	JANUARY 3, 1969, KERPEN, GERMANY
Website	www.michael-schumacher.de
Teams	JORDAN 1991
	BENETTON 1991–1995
	FERRARI 1996–2002

A Winner Again: Michael became the driver with the most Grand Prix wins to his name in 2001, hitting 53

It's easy to run out of superlatives when describing Michael's driving, as he's a master of making his car go where he wants. The records support this, too, as he holds the record number of wins. But what really marks him out is his unceasing effort to be the best. He may be the world's highest-paid sportsman, with £45 million coming his way in 2003 and 2004, but he's always ready to test racing cars rather than spending time on a yacht.

A challenger whatever the equipment, Michael trounced his opponents last year as he was, for once, armed with the most competitive car. His rivals must be quaking, as there's every chance that he'll enjoy a similar situation this year.

Michael won the first two races of last year. However, although his win in Malaysia demonstrated his wet-weather skills, it owed something to fortune as he went out on intermediate tyres while everyone else fitted wets, with intermediates proving the ones to have.

Michael received a wake-up call when Montoya jumped him in Brazil. Coulthard also got past – on a wet track, too. Yet, if Michael didn't win, he almost always came second. Luck played its part too, such as In Spain when Hakkinen's car failed with half a lap to go, and in Monaco when poleman Coulthard stalled on the grid. He even had the new experience of tussling with younger brother Ralf, but when the moment was right, he would win, as at the Nurburgring and Magny-Cours. Michael wrapped up the title at the Hungaroring, with four races still to run.

Michael was out of sorts at Monza, affected by that week's terrorist attacks on the USA. Back at his imperious best in the Japanese GP, Michael reminded his rivals that they'll need to step up a gear to challenge him in 2002.

CAREER RECORD

First Grand Prix	1991 BELGIAN GP
Grand Prix starts	162
Grand Prix wins	53

1992 Belgian GP, 1993 Portuguese GP, 1994 Brazilian GP, Pacific GP, San Marino GP, Monaco GP, Canadian GP, French GP, Hungarian GP, European GP, 1995 Brazilian GP, Spanish GP, Monaco GP, French GP, German GP, Belgian GP, European GP, Pacific GP, Japanese GP, 1996 Spanish GP, Belgian GP, Italian GP, 1997 Monaco GP, Canadian GP, French GP, Belgian GP, Japanese GP, 1998 Argentinian GP, Canadian GP, French GP, British GP, Hungarian GP, Italian GP, 1999 San Marino GP, Monaco GP, 2000 Australian GP, Brazilian GP, San Marino GP, European GP, Canadian GP, Italian GP, US GP, Japanese GP, Malaysian GP, 2001 Australian GP, Malaysian GP, Spanish GP, Monaco GP, European GP, French GP, Hungarian GP, Belgian GP, Japanese GP

Poles	43
Fastest laps	43
Points	801
Honours	2001, 2000, 1995, & 1994 FORMULA ONE CHAMPION, 1998 FORMULA ONE RUNNER-UP, 1990 GERMAN FORMULA THREE CHAMPION & MACAU GP WINNER, 1988 GERMAN FORMULA KONIG CHAMPION

Fast from the start

Being the son of a kart circuit owner was a great start, and Michael made the most of it. He rocketed through the first two rungs of German single-seaters in just one season and then made an impact in Formula Three in 1989. Picked up by Mercedes, he gained valuable experience in sportscars, but then a chance opening at Jordan in 1991 gave him his Formula One break and Michael hasn't looked back, winning two titles with Benetton and then taking Ferrari back to glory in 2000 after a near miss in 1998.

RUBENS BARRICHELLO

GETTING EVER STRONGER

Last year was probably the year in which Rubens Barrichello came of age as a driver. He'd won once before, but this time he got closer to Michael Schumacher than ever before. Expect wins in 2002.

Valued Number Two: Rubens stretched his legs in 2001 and scored a hatful of points for Ferrari but never a race win

Rubens is famed for letting his emotions mask his talents behind the wheel. However, as last year progressed, it was clear that he's letting his head do the talking rather than his heart. Should this trend continue, he may, after all, move into the position to take over from Michael Schumacher as Ferrari's undisputed number one when the great man retires.

Although Rubens bagged a third, then a second behind Schumacher at the start of last year, his second with Ferrari, the pressure of it all, including talk of him losing his Ferrari ride for 2002, got to him on his home ground when he collided with Ralf Schumacher. Although Ferrari wasn't on it at Imola, Rubens claimed third. But then came the race that made it clear that his role at Ferrari was that of back-up. This was the Austrian GP when he was told to stop chasing leader Coulthard to let a recovering Schumacher through. For several laps he failed to respond, rendering team director Jean Todt apoplectic, before doing so at the finish. Differences with the team were patched up, though, as Ferrari signed Rubens for 2002 before the next grand prix.

A smattering of seconds and thirds filled his summer, but it was only once Schumacher had landed the title that Rubens was let off the leash, with Michael saying that he'd do all he could to help him finish as runner-up, even if that meant letting Rubens through to win. Rubens said that "it was unusual to be in a position to have Michael help me, rather than coming to a race to help him. But I have to be competitive so that he can help me, as it's no use if I'm running fifth and he's leading..." And so it proved, despite very strong runs at Monza and Indianapolis.

However, there was praise from within, with Ross Brawn saying that if the car is bad, then he considers Rubens as capable as Michael of getting a decent race out of it. Over one lap, though, he reckons that Michael has the edge.

A quick learner

Rubens hit the ground running when he arrived in Europe, waltzing to the 1990 European Formula Opel title. He beat David Coulthard to the 1991 British Formula Three crown, but although he took third overall in Formula 3000 in 1992, it was only when he reached Formula One with Jordan in 1993 that people sat up and paid attention. For he ran second behind Ayrton Senna in only his third grand prix. His car broke at the end, but the impression was made. Jordan wasn't a match for Williams and Benetton, though, and second place in the 1995 Canadian GP remained his best until he left Stewart after a three-year stint and joined Ferrari in 2000, going on to win that year's German GP.

TRACK NOTES

Nationality	**BRAZILIAN**
Born	**MAY 23, 1972,**
	SAO PAULO, BRAZIL
Website	**www.barrichello.com.br**
Teams	**JORDAN 1993–1996**
	STEWART 1997–1999
	FERRARI 2000–2002

CAREER RECORD

First Grand Prix	1993
	SOUTH AFRICAN GP
Grand Prix starts	147
Grand Prix wins	1
	2000 German GP
Poles	3
Fastest laps	3
Points	195
Honours	**1991 BRITISH FORMULA THREE CHAMPION,**
	1990 EUROPEAN FORMULA OPEL CHAMPION, 1988 BRAZILIAN KART CHAMPION

McLAREN

ANXIOUS TO BOUNCE BACK

McLaren and Mercedes have spent the winter working flat-out to make sure that they'll offer a stronger challenge to Ferrari than they did last year. The only change is Kimi Räikkönen filling the seat vacated by the 'resting' Mika Hakkinen.

The Boss: Ron Dennis had a great deal on his mind during the 2001 season, but you can be sure that absolutely no stone will have been left unturned in his and McLaren's quest for success in 2002

When you think of McLaren, you think of success in Formula One. You look at their silver cars and you think professionalism. You look at their demeanour and it's serious. McLaren is a team dedicated to winning: think of the runaway days of the 1980s, when the team's drivers claimed six titles in a seven-year run, and also Hakkinen's reign in the late 1990s. But, the sport is cyclical and McLaren is going to have to pull out all the stops to make sure that it doesn't slip away and leave Ferrari and Williams to fight over the spoils.

However, nothing motivates McLaren as much as failure. While last year's tally of four wins from 17 races would please the majority of teams, it didn't please McLaren. Add to that the fact that some insiders were talking of the battle for honours being fought out between Ferrari and Williams in 2002, and you can imagine how much midnight oil will have been burned at their Woking headquarters since the end of last season to ensure that McLaren is up there with them.

But McLaren isn't a team to panic, and its team principal Ron Dennis, a man who

famously said that he would wake in pain in the morning after a grand prix if one of his cars hadn't won, said: "I believe that it's a measure of the strength of our organisation that we've conditioned ourselves to respond to success and disappointment with a sense of balance and perspective."

One of the keys to McLaren's success is stability. Its sponsors stay for record-breaking stints, aiding continuity in appearance. So do its engine suppliers – Mercedes has been part of the package since 1995 – and so do its staff and drivers. However, Formula One's longest-lasting driver partnership has now been broken up. Mika Hakkinen and David Coulthard will not be driving together for the seventh consecutive year, as Hakkinen has elected to take a year out, opening the way for 2001 sensation Kimi Räikkönen. Hakkinen talked of returning in 2003, but few expect him to do so. Indeed, if he did, Dennis would have too many drivers on his books, with Coulthard, Räikkönen and third driver Alexander Wurz signed up, as well as Hakkinen, all jousting for two race seats.

The choice of Räikkönen to stand in for or, probably, replace Hakkinen is a logical one, as he hit Formula One with a bang last year. Most people didn't even know who he was, as the young Finn hadn't raced in Formula 3000 or even in Formula Three, but he'd done enough to impress Peter Sauber. Räikkönen was given a licence grudgingly by the sport's governing body due to his lack of experience. But the requirement for him to be officially observed during the first four races was thrown into ridicule when he finished sixth on his debut. More points followed, although by the end of the year he appeared to be trying too hard and his form dropped back behind that of his team-mate Nick Heidfeld – a driver with long associations with both McLaren and Mercedes. However, it was Räikkönen who was picked, perhaps as much as anything to prevent Ferrari from signing a potential future champion. Whether the choice is the right one remains to be seen, especially with regard to how Räikkönen fits in with the Woking Way Of Doing Things. As it is, Hakkinen reckons that Räikkönen will learn a great deal from Coulthard, and may even pick up a win this year.

Coulthard is sure to be in the thick of the fight, as he drove beautifully last year, although the sting was taken out of his tail by mechanical failures, especially after the reintroduction of traction control and the introduction of launch control. Witness his frustration on the grid when he stalled at Monaco and undid his herculean efforts in securing pole.

As ever, Dennis is adamant that McLaren never uses team orders. "We don't have number one status and never have had. We will provide both drivers with equal equipment and the outcome will be the outcome," said Dennis. Mind you, Coulthard discovered last year the advantage of being the team-mate with more points.

To challenge Ferrari and Williams, Mercedes has changed from an engine with a 90 degree V-angle to one of 72 degrees and must hope that this will provide Coulthard and Räikkönen with more horsepower; and Dennis must hope that the team's move from Bridgestone to Michelin rubber means that their tyres are the ones to have. And all at McLaren must hope that Ferrari have driven into a technical cul-de-sac.

Flying Scot: David Coulthard became a really potent weapon for McLaren in 2001, pushing Michael Schumacher hard until the season's mid-point

A mixed year

Mixed Conditions: Sometimes in 2001 the sun didn't shine on McLaren

Last year's McLaren MP4-16 was clearly fragile when it came to its launch control, but it had good traction and had been designed to run with a larger fuel tank than that of the Ferraris, offering more scope for race tactics. Indeed, McLaren had the upper hand in this department, but they lost out in terms of both power and handling. Indeed, the team struggled with its MP4-16, suffering by having to run to a high-nose design and lagging behind its rivals as a result of having less pre-season testing.

McLaren was then rattled in the first round by Ferrari's form, but if Hakkinen's suspension hadn't failed, he'd have had a very good chance of winning in Melbourne, as he'd been running a longer fuel strategy than Michael Schumacher.

The deluge that swept across Sepang wrote off McLaren's chances when the Ferrari drivers were blessed by their team's decision to send them out on intermediate tyres rather than wets, though Coulthard still collected four points. However, McLaren's decision to send its drivers into the Brazilian GP with their cars set up for wet conditions was a masterstroke, and Coulthard duly ended Ferrari's six-race winning streak.

It seems Coulthard has never been able to feel highly thought-of at McLaren, but the form that took him into a share of the championship lead after four rounds – including his exemplary win in Brazil and his pursuit of Ralf Schumacher at Imola – ought to have made him feel that he was progressing. However, Dennis showed his colours after Coulthard's car was unable to get away in the Spanish GP thus dropping him to the rear of the grid, accusing the Scot of "brain fade". This was at the first race where the start was effectively out of the drivers' hands due to the introduction of launch control, and it proved to be a computer glitch rather than Coulthard's fault. Notably, Dennis wasn't so quick to apportion blame when Hakkinen stalled in Brazil or in Austria. Perhaps Dennis was simply upset in Spain that Hakkinen had been denied victory when his car failed with half a lap to go.

Victory for Coulthard in Austria gave him a 34-point advantage over Hakkinen, yet Dennis refused to force Hakkinen to support his challenge. He did, however, hint that Coulthard would be kept on for 2002...

It was around this time that news broke that Adrian Newey might be taking his design skills to Jaguar. McLaren enticed him to stay with the promise of other projects, including designing a yacht to tackle the Americas Cup.

McLaren was hit by another bombshell at Monaco when Hakkinen asked for a year's sabbatical, to spend time with wife Erja and son Hugo. The race brought heartache for Coulthard, who earned a superb pole position but had his launch control fail at the start of the parade lap, and was forced to start from the back of the grid. Failure

FOR THE RECORD

Country of origin	England
Team base	Woking, England
Website	www.mclaren.com
Active in Formula One	From 1966
Grands Prix contested	526
Wins	134
Pole positions	112
Fastest laps	107

DRIVERS + RESULTS 2001

Driver	Nationality	Races	Wins	Pts	Pos
David Coulthard	Scottish	17	2	65	2nd
Mika Hakkinen	Finnish	17	2	37	5th

CAR SPECIFICATIONS

Team principal	Ron Dennis
Technical director	Adrian Newey
Team manager	David Ryan
Chief designer	Neil Oatley
Chief engineer	Steve Hallam
Test driver	Alexander Wurz
Chassis	McLaren MP4-17
Engine	Mercedes V10
Tyres	Michelin

to pass Bernoldi's Arrows for 42 laps delayed him so much that his recovery drive got him only as far as fifth.

McLaren failed to match Ferrari and Williams mid-season, but when the weather conditions were cold or wet it was clear that Bridgestone provided a better tyre. This was shown at the British GP as they qualified second and third, and Hakkinen won as he pleased, with Coulthard ruing a first-corner clash with Trulli. Then, apart from second in the Belgian GP, the next few races had McLaren playing a supporting role. But it came right for Mika at Indianapolis as he scored another win to take into his sabbatical. However, this had looked unlikely when the lap that had put him second on the grid was scrapped for passing a red light at the pitlane exit in the warm-up. His second fastest qualifying lap was good only for fourth on the grid, but it's said that his subsequent fury helped focus his mind.

A team of winners

McLaren is a British team, but its founder wasn't, for Bruce McLaren was a Kiwi. The youngest-ever grand prix winner when he won the 1959 United States GP at the age of 22, Bruce went on to build his own cars, entering one for the first time in 1966. McLaren's first win came in 1968 and its first drivers' and constructors' titles in 1974 thanks to Emerson Fittipaldi. James Hunt was champion in 1976, but it was only after Dennis took over in 1980 that the team hit the front again. Niki Lauda topped the points table in 1984, then Alain Prost in 1985, 1986 and 1989, with Ayrton Senna doing the honours in 1988, 1990 and 1991. After being outstripped by Williams in the mid-1990s, Hakkinen was champion in 1998 and 1999.

Support Act: Test driver Alex Wurz's input was valuable

DAVID COULTHARD

HE MEANS BUSINESS

David Coulthard stepped up a gear last year, sharpened his focus and, some say, made the most of Mika Hakkinen's loss of form as he finished second. If McLaren can provide him with a better car this year, he could really fight for honours.

David knows that, for the first time since joining McLaren in 1996, he'll start the season as the team's nominal number one driver. Sure, the team has a policy of not having a number two, but it has tended to favour one over the other and, this time, that driver will be David, unless Kimi Räikkönen is immediately on the pace. David knows, too, that only a less-than-competitive car will slow him, as long as his new-found consistent excellence continues. On the evidence of 2001, though, there's a possibility that he may not have the ultimate machinery.

Ferrari's dominant form in 2001's opening races suggested that the title would elude him, yet David was on the podium at both, then not only won in Brazil, but outraced Michael Schumacher. More importantly, it put him – rather than team-mate Mika Hakkinen – in the dominant position in the team.

David was the first driver to be hampered by the arrival of launch control when his engine stalled in Spain. Had he not been forced to start from the back of the grid, he'd probably have won. Instead, he finished fifth after damaging his car's nose. He then won in Austria by dint of clever tactics that sent him out with a heavy fuel load.

David's finest lap was the one that took pole at Monaco, but that was wasted when his car again stalled on the parade lap. This was later described as "not being a launch control but a systems failure". That his fortune started to wane is shown by the fact that he was four points down on Schumacher after six rounds and yet ended up 58 adrift after 17. Indeed, of the six races from Canada to Hungary, David picked up only two thirds and a fourth.

In the closing four races, once Schumacher had brought an end to David's slim chance of overhauling him, Coulthard was quoted as saying that he wasn't interested in finishing as runner-up. But he clarified this, saying that it wasn't a case of him not being interested, but more that "his motivation wasn't to finish second", like in any race.

The flying Scotsman

It took David just one year from turning his back on a hugely successful karting career to land a Formula One test. This came the Scottish teenager's way in 1990 after a stunning season of Formula Ford in 1989 as a prize put up by McLaren and *Autosport* magazine. Inspired, David pushed Rubens Barrichello hard in the 1991 British Formula Three season. Although fast in Formula 3000, David appeared on the verge of running out of money. Indeed, he was fortunate that he was Williams' test driver in 1994, and even more so, though in tragic circumstances, when he was promoted to the race team after Ayrton Senna's death. A winner in 1995, David moved to McLaren in 1996 and helped them rediscover their winning ways in 1997. More wins followed each year, but until 2001 he was in Hakkinen's shadow.

Broad Smile: David Coulthard was sensational in Brazil

TRACK NOTES

Nationality	SCOTTISH
Born	MARCH 27, 1971,
	TWYNHOLM, SCOTLAND
Website	
	www.davidcoulthard.co.uk
Teams	1994–1995 WILLIAMS
	1996–2002 McLAREN

CAREER RECORD

First Grand Prix	1994 SPANISH GP
Grand Prix starts	124
Grand Prix wins	11
	1995 Portuguese GP,
	1997 Australian GP, Italian GP,
	1998 San Marino GP,
	1999 British GP, Belgian GP,
	2000 British GP,
	Monaco GP, French GP,
	2001 Brazilian GP, Austrian GP
Poles	12
Fastest laps	17
Points	359
Honours	
	2001 FORMULA ONE RUNNER-UP,
	1991 BRITISH FORMULA THREE
	RUNNER-UP & MACAU GP WINNER,
	1989 McLAREN AUTOSPORT YOUNG
	DRIVER OF THE YEAR & BRITISH
	JUNIOR FORMULA FORD CHAMPION,
	1988 SCOTTISH KART CHAMPION

KIMI RÄIKKÖNEN

THE NEW FLYING FINN

If you had told people just over a year ago that Kimi Räikkönen would race in Formula One, no one would have believed you. That this will be his second season, and that it will be with McLaren, makes it all the more amazing. He has to make the most of this opportunity.

Looking Ahead: Kimi is 100% driven, which is precisely how McLaren want him for 2002

Kimi starts 2002 with just 40 car races behind him. Yet, if the raw speed he displayed last year is harnessed to full effect, he should be a regular visitor to the podium – perhaps even to the top step. The pressure on him will be even greater, as whatever he did that was good last year was a bonus, yet this year it will be expected.

The Finnish press describes Kimi as the "Peter Pan" of Formula One. His approach to his driving is impressive, but he can tend to rebel against authority, something that won't impress team principal Ron Dennis.

It was known that Ferrari saw Kimi as perhaps Michael Schumacher's natural successor. However, after Hakkinen asked for a sabbatical, McLaren got busy. Sauber

wasn't keen to release Kimi from his three-year contract, but £13.5 million convinced them. Kimi's deal is for one year, with options for more, pending Hakkinen's return.

Asked how he'd feel to have Mika helping him, Kimi said: "It's going to be helpful if somebody like Mika who knows the team can help me." But his message was clear that he'll soon be seeking no guidance. The pressure at McLaren, it was pointed out, would be more than at Sauber. Kimi batted that one back: "McLaren Is expecting a lot from me, but I had to make a big leap last year, coming from Formula Renault to Formula One, so I think that the pressure won't be any greater."

The FIA's monitoring of Kimi In the first four grands prix was shown to be unnecessary after he scored a point at his first attempt, in which he was only 12 seconds and two positions behind team-mate Nick Heidfeld in Melbourne. Yet his performance at Imola was the one that marked his arrival, as he outqualified Heidfeld then kept up with the Ferraris, until he crashed when his steering wheel came off. Kimi finished fourth in Austria and Canada, then fifth at Silverstone, but the rest of his year was marked by accidents – even though the one at Suzuka was thought to be due to mechanical failure – and many suggested he had taken his eye off the ball. Or perhaps Sauber was no longer focused on the driver who had turned his back on them.

Rising like a shot

Karting hotshot Kimi was snapped up by Steve Robertson, whose father David promotes

Jenson Button. Entered in the British Formula Renault series in 1999, Kimi was third on his debut, but Robertson pulled him out when it was clear that his rivals had superior cars. Back for the Formula Renault winter series, Kimi won all four races. Signed up by the strongest team, Manor Motorsport, he won the 2000 title but, just when people thought he'd be heading for Formula Three in 2001, Robertson landed him a test with Sauber, and this was enough for Peter Sauber to propel him past Formula 3000 too.

TRACK NOTES

Nationality	FINNISH
Born	OCTOBER 17, 1979,
	ESPOO, FINLAND
Website	www.kimiraikkonen.com
Teams	SAUBER 2001
	McLAREN 2002

CAREER RECORD

First Grand Prix	2001
	AUSTRALIAN GP
Grand Prix starts	17
Grand Prix wins	0
	(best result: fourth,
	2001 Austrian & Canadian GP)
Poles	0
Fastest laps	0
Points	9
Honours	2000 BRITISH
	FORMULA RENAULT CHAMPION,
	1999 BRITISH FORMULA RENAULT
	WINTER SERIES CHAMPION,
	1998 EUROPEAN SUPER A KART
	RUNNER-UP & FINNISH KART
	CHAMPION & NORDIC KART
	CHAMPION

>> WILLIAMS

IN FLYING FORM

On last year's form, Williams and BMW could be back at the top again in 2002, ahead of Ferrari, with fans the world over also watching out for an internal battle for supremacy between team-mates Juan Pablo Montoya and Ralf Schumacher.

SIR FRANK WILLIAMS

After racing in Formula Three, Frank ran Piers Courage in Formula One in 1969. A thin time followed Courage's death in 1970, but securing Saudi Arabian backing in the late 1970s transformed his team's fortunes, with wins flowing since 1979. He has been confined to a wheelchair since a car crash in France in 1986.

PATRICK HEAD

Son of a racer, Patrick used his engineering qualifications to good effect with Lola before joining Wolf-Williams in 1976. A founder of Williams Grand Prix Engineering with Frank in 1977, he runs the technical side of the team, managing the operations as much as the design side.

If you want sparks between team-mates, look no further than Williams. All through last year there was an icy atmosphere in their pit, almost as though there was an invisible barrier between the team's established driver Ralf Schumacher and newcomer Juan Pablo Montoya. You could count on one hand how many times they were seen talking together away from team debriefs. They were like chalk and cheese – both waiting to break into the winner's circle, but one perhaps overhyped by the media and the other getting fed up with this adulation without solid results.

Team principal Sir Frank Williams has always liked to have real racers as his drivers, so the internal tension amused him and, no doubt, kept the drivers on their toes. However, technical director Patrick Head says that no friction has arisen between the two as the result of something that happened out on the track, and that if there is any friction, then it's just something fuelled by the media. Friction or not, Head said: "I'd rather have two quick guys in the team than one quick one and one slow one."

Don't forget, though, that Williams ran two quick guys who didn't like each other back in 1986 – Nigel Mansell and Nelson Piquet – and their intra-team fighting allowed McLaren's Alain Prost to sneak through to take the title.

So, Williams has race winners in Montoya and Schumacher. It's also likely to have the most powerful engines if BMW can continue the advances made through 2001. Tyre supplier Michelin will also have more experience of all conditions after a successful first season back in the sport's top echelon, though they were occasionally caught out by changing conditions. Indeed, the fact that their tyres had different performance characteristics from the Bridgestones, and came good at different times, made for more interesting viewing. There was a question-mark over the team's tactics, as they often fell short of the excellence of those employed by Ferrari and McLaren, but you can be sure that these will improve.

The final part of the equation is how good the chassis is going to be in reality, but Gavin Fisher and Geoff Willis produced a nimble chassis last year so, with no rule changes for 2002, there's every reason to believe that they'll do so again. However, aerodynamicist Willis won't be staying to help develop the chassis beyond the start of March as he's moving to BAR.

Getting better and better

Earmarked as a team that would race nearer the front than they had in 2000, Williams didn't disappoint. It was a sure bet that BMW would provide a belter of an engine for its second year back after a conservative reintroduction in 2000. It was also likely that

Powerful Trio: Team owner Sir Frank Williams is flanked by BMW Motorsport chief Gerhard Berger and by Ralf Schumacher, a combination that helped Williams and BMW win again

22

Going for Gold: Ralf Schumacher became a winner for Williams in 2001 and then followed this up by winning twice more before the year was out

the FW23 chassis would be competitive. However, no one was sure whether their decision to run on Michelin tyres would be a help or a hindrance. Wonderful tyres for qualifying were considered likely, judging by Michelin's previous spell in Formula One, but their competitiveness in the races wasn't as definite. Michelin's lack of ability in cold weather was shown in a cold and wet practice at the San Marino GP, yet Ralf bounced back to win the race...

There had already been a clear sign that the Michelins were good in race trim, however, as Montoya had led the Brazilian GP until being taken out by Arrows driver Jos Verstappen just after lapping him. And this famous run included passing and then pulling away from Michael Schumacher's Ferrari, which was running with a fuel load that was thought to be around 40kg lighter... Notably, Ralf set by far the fastest lap that day after an early pit stop following his second clash in a row with Barrichello.

The general consensus was that the BMW engine was the most powerful of all, pushing out more than 840bhp, some 20bhp more than the next most-blessed operators, Ferrari. The Mercedes and Cosworth engines were a further 10bhp down, and the early-season Renault said to be as much as 100bhp down before it made great strides in the second half of the season. Furthermore, the Williams FW23 was aerodynamically efficient, something that reaped dividends when combined with its ample BMW horsepower. However, it required a lot of wing to produce downforce.

Another strength was that the FW23 had been designed to carry a larger-than-average fuel tank, and this gave them more scope for amending their race tactics, especially when jousting with the smaller-tanked Ferraris.

If Williams and BMW partied in Melbourne in 2000 when Ralf gave them third place on their first race together, then that was nothing in comparison with the way in which they celebrated at Imola last year when Ralf started third. He grabbed the lead from the start by blasting past the McLarens and was never headed, giving Williams its first win since the 1997 Luxembourg GP and BMW its first since one of its engines powered BMW's current motorsport boss, Gerhard Berger, to victory in the 1986 Mexican GP.

Head was less than happy to have to change the car's diffuser after the Spanish GP, Ferrari having convinced the FIA that the diffuser Williams had been using – and which had approved by the FIA some 18 months earlier – was outside the spirit of the regulations. That Spanish GP yielded a fortunate second place for Juan Pablo, but the FW23s were surprisingly off the pace of the McLarens and Ferraris here. However, the cars looked good next time out at the A1-Ring – in qualifying at least, as this time their Michelin rubber was no match for the Bridgestones in the race itself. But Juan Pablo gave the team more time in the limelight by leading for the first 15 laps before clashing with Michael Schumacher. Notably, both Ralf and Juan Pablo showed in this race that the team had sorted its new launch control system to good effect, as both rocketed past the pole-sitting Ferrari driver at the start.

Montoya learned a useful lesson mid-season when he crashed in both Monaco and Canada while pushing too hard. Sir Frank called him in for a chat and his driving became less ragged thereafter. Indeed, Sir Frank joked later that "the wall hit him".

Canada wasn't all bad for Williams, though, as Ralf got the better of his brother after a lengthy fight for his second win. He could then have made it two in a row, but he was penalised for crossing the line at the pit exit at the Nürburgring and the penalty dropped him to fourth. Juan Pablo claimed only his second finish of the season and was second.

Signs of internal team discontent seemed to surface in the next two races, with Ralf not appearing to be impressed by Juan Pablo's improving form and refusing to let him pass at Magny-Cours – even though the two drivers were running to different tactics. He did the same thing at Silverstone, too.

Ralf triumphed in the German GP, but it should have been Juan Pablo's race. Unfortunately, Montoya was slowed by a fuel-rig failure that delayed him in the pits and, as a result, his engine overheated and failed soon afterwards.

A breakthrough came at the Belgian GP with the introduction of scalloped sidepods. If both cars hadn't ended up dropping from the front row to the tail of the field at Spa-Francorchamps, then they could possibly have won the race. Montoya then controlled the Italian GP, led the US GP and pressed Michael Schumacher all the way in Japan.

The team had to hold its hand up to errors, however, such as when Ralf's car was still on blocks having adjustments made to its rear wing when the mechanics had to leave the grid before the parade lap for the restart of the Belgian GP... BMW and the team bosses used this as a stick with which to beat the team, so expect to see a more tightly-drilled team turning up in Melbourne.

The team's Achilles heel was its finishing record: at 16 out of a possible 34 chequered flags for the two drivers combined, it was the equal worst tally in F1, level with Jaguar and Minardi. The drivers should hang their heads, too, as mechanical failures only just outnumbered retirements through spins and accidents. Engine failures stemmed from BMW pushing the tolerance levels of its components to the maximum in their quest for power.

From rags to riches

Frank Williams served a long apprenticeship in Formula One before his team joined the ranks of winners in 1979. He first ran Piers Courage in a Brabham in 1969, and then in a de Tomaso in 1970. But Piers was killed that year, and the only highlight of the following years was Jacques Laffite's second place in the 1975 German GP. Forming Williams Grand Prix Engineering in 1977 with Patrick Head and landing substantial backing transformed matters, and Alan Jones was a regular winner in 1979 before becoming their first champion in 1980. Keke Rosberg, Nelson Piquet, Nigel Mansell, Alain Prost, Damon Hill and Jacques Villeneuve have all been champions since, but the loss of works Renault engines at the end of 1997 dropped Williams from the top until BMW came along for 2000.

Pure Delight: Every member of the BMWWilliamsF1 race crew celebrates from the pit wall as Ralf Schumacher sweeps past to victory in the Canadian GP

FOR THE RECORD

Country of origin	England
Team base	Grove, England
Website	www.bmwwilliamsf1.com
Active in Formula One	From 1977
Grands Prix contested	445
Wins	107
Pole positions	112
Fastest laps	119

DRIVERS + RESULTS 2001

Driver	Nationality	Races	Wins	Pts	Pos
Juan Pablo Montoya	Colombian	17	1	31	6th
Ralf Schumacher	German	17	3	49	4th

CAR SPECIFICATIONS

Team principal	Sir Frank Williams
Technical director	Patrick Head
Team manager	Dickie Stanford
Chief designer	Gavin Fisher
Chief engineer	Sam Michael
Test drivers	Marc Gene & Antonio Pizzonia
Chassis	Williams FW24
Engine	BMW V10
Tyres	Michelin

RALF SCHUMACHER

Ralf Schumacher knows that if he drives at his best this year he could have a chance of becoming the second Schumacher to win the Formula One title. But first he has to beat his team-mate.

Victory Vee: Ralf Schumacher celebrates winning on home ground in the German GP at Hockenheim

Ralf has a fight on his hands, a fight for supremacy within Williams. This will be brought to him by Juan Pablo Montoya. How Ralf stands up to the challenge will be one of the year's talking points.

Ralf won three times last year to Montoya's single victory, but the Colombian had the upper hand at the season's end and Ralf was quick to request that Williams focus on one driver. However, BMW motorsport boss Gerhard Berger criticised Ralf: "It was the wrong time to say it. If you look at the last four races, the team would have to concentrate on Montoya."

Yet, if Ralf harnesses his skills to achieve the maximum in 2002, and Williams, BMW and Michelin come up trumps with chassis, engine and tyres respectively, there's no reason why he shouldn't end up as the first sibling to win a world title.

Ralf started 2001 armed with the most powerful engine combined with an effective chassis. He was tipped into a spin by Barrichello twice in the first three races, but then came the San Marino GP in which Ralf turned a third place on the grid into the lead by the first corner, going on to score his first win. If his win at Imola was momentous, his win in Canada was more satisfying as it involved beating his brother fair and square. Yet hopes of glory next time out at the Nürburgring were scuppered when Michael forced him towards the pitwall on the run to the first corner.

For all his success, it became apparent at Magny-Cours that not all the team were fond of Ralf. It was said that this was because he had not thanked them after winning at Imola or Montreal. Their affection for Montoya was also more obvious.

Ralf's third win came in the German GP, a race that he inherited when Montoya suffered a delayed pit stop. Then Ralf was exasperated in Belgium when adjustments on the grid weren't completed in time and his car was left on blocks when the mechanics had to leave the grid, scuppering his pole for the restart. Being outraced by Montoya in each of the last three races will have made Ralf think long and hard over the winter.

Proving himself

When Ralf graduated from karts in 1992, everyone wanted to see whether Michael's younger brother had the same talent. Ralf didn't, but he was a winner in German Formula Three in 1994, going on to be runner-up in 1995, also winning the Macau Formula Three race.

He proved his supporters right, though, when he became Formula Nippon champion at his first attempt in 1996.

Ralf then impressed when he made his Formula One debut with Jordan in 1997, but had a string of accidents. He felt aggrieved that he wasn't allowed to challenge team-mate Hill for victory in the 1998 Belgian GP and left for Williams in 1999, only a puncture denying him a win at the Nürburgring.

TRACK NOTES

Nationality	**GERMAN**
Born	**JUNE 30, 1975,**
	KERPEN, GERMANY
Website	**www.ralf-schumacher.de**
Teams	**JORDAN 1997–1998**
	WILLIAMS 1999–2002

CAREER RECORD

First Grand Prix	**1997**
	AUSTRALIAN GP
Grand Prix starts	**83**
Grand Prix wins	**3**
	2001 San Marino GP,
	Canadian GP, German GP
Poles	**1**
Fastest laps	**6**
Points	**135**
Honours	**1996 FORMULA**
	NIPPON CHAMPION,
	1995 GERMAN FORMULA THREE
	RUNNER-UP & MACAU GP WINNER,
	1993 GERMAN FORMEL
	JUNIOR RUNNER-UP

JUAN PABLO MONTOYA

READY TO STRIKE

Juan Pablo Montoya became a winner last year and he could have won several times more. More than this, though, the Colombian laid down his marker with both Schumachers, and is tipped by many as a likely world champion.

The person a driver must beat above all others is their team-mate. Juan Pablo knows that, and if you want evidence of his rivalry with Ralf Schumacher, you only had to witness a photo-call at last year's United States GP. Posing with a baseball great who handed the drivers a baseball bat each, Ralf admired his while Juan Pablo aimed a pretend blow at Ralf's head...

Juan Pablo qualified poorly in Melbourne but demonstrated his rocket-like starts, passing six cars before the first corner. He then ran across the grass, but demonstrated this ability again before launch control was introduced at the Spanish GP. However, he'd have traded these starts for a finish in any of the first four races. Cruellest of his retirements came in Brazil after he'd suggested a redefinition of the world order was imminent, when he forced his way past Michael Schumacher and was pulling away, until he was taken out by a driver he'd just lapped – Verstappen.

The Spanish GP yielded second when Hakkinen retired on the last lap. Then Juan Pablo led the Austrian GP until he defended his line from Michael Schumacher and ran both of them off the road. Again, his car was to fail, but he'd got Michael rattled, even though certain drivers thought that he needed to calm down.

Mistakes in Monaco and Canada blotted his copybook, as he hit the barriers in both races. However, he appeared to learn that less haste can mean more speed, and next led a Grand Prix in Germany – until his pit-stop turned into farce. On rejoining the race, his engine blew as a result of overheating during the over-long stop.

Juan Pablo started to get the better of Ralf as a result of "raising his game",

according to team chief Patrick Head. However, he wasted pole for the Belgian GP by stalling on the grid. But that long-expected first win came at the Italian GP, with strong showings in the final two races – only engine failure beat him in the USA, and Michael Schumacher in Japan.

Summing up the year, Juan Pablo said: "I broke down nine or ten times, and in about eight of those I was in the points, which makes it really tough."

TRACK NOTES

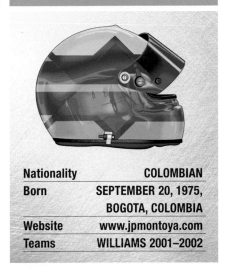

Nationality	COLOMBIAN
Born	SEPTEMBER 20, 1975, BOGOTA, COLOMBIA
Website	www.jpmontoya.com
Teams	WILLIAMS 2001–2002

CAREER RECORD

First Grand Prix	2001 AUSTRALIAN GP
Grand Prix starts	17
Grand Prix wins	1 2001 Italian GP
Poles	3
Fastest laps	3
Points	31
Honours	2000 INDY 500 WINNER, 1999 INDYCAR CHAMPION, 1998 FORMULA 3000 CHAMPION

Reason to Smile: Juan Pablo Montoya came, saw and eventually conquered at Monza in a truly impressive first season of Formula One

Always abroad

Juan Pablo left Colombia to race in the USA in 1994, then moved from the Barber Dodge Pro-Series to Formula Vauxhall in Britain in 1995. Using the less-competitive Mitsubishi engines hampered his 1996 Formula Three campaign, but he impressed in Formula 3000 in 1997. Indeed, he should have been champion, but too many accidents hurt his chances. After winning the title in 1998, Juan Pablo found that there was no opening for him to move up from Williams' test team to its race team, so he headed to Indycars and raced to the title. The highlight of his 2000 season was winning the Indy 500.

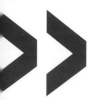

SAUBER

THE ONLY WAY IS DOWN

Sauber was delighted to be the fourth most successful team last year, but believed this was as much due to the failure of other midfield teams as to their own progress, and they can only hope that they'll finish as highly placed again.

Up With The Big Boys: Nick Heidfeld joined Michael Schumacher and David Coulthard on the podium after finishing a career-best third overall in the Brazilian GP. It was the year that the team came of age

Peter Sauber is hoping that lightning will strike twice as, for the second year running, he's introducing a relative unknown into his team's second seat, with Felipe Massa following Kimi Räikkönen.

As soon as news broke that Räikkönen was off to McLaren, with McLaren and Mercedes paying an alleged £13.5 million to release him from his contract, Massa's name came into the frame. Insiders asked, "Who?", but inspection revealed that the 20-year-old Brazilian was setting the pace in the second-division Euro Formula 3000 series after

clinching the European Formula Renault crown in 2000. Indeed, a victory the following weekend helped him clinch the title.

Sauber was clear about his reasons for picking the Brazilian: "We've again opted for a talented young driver. He convinced us with his excellent performances during tests at Mugello." Sauber also said that Räikkönen was a very good driver, but an egotistical one and "not necessarily a nice one".

Having been passed over by McLaren, for whom he'd been test driver in 1998 and 1999, Nick Heidfeld will be even more fired

up this year as he believes that he's a better prospect than his former team-mate.

The fact that Sauber will continue to use Petronas-badged Ferrari engines, last year's works Ferrari engines, means that the drivers will have plenty of horsepower. They'll both be praying that the C21 proves as effective a package. With a new wind tunnel, it ought to.

Sauber's cars will look different this year, as the symbol of sponsor Red Bull is expected to be missing from its livery for the first time since 1995, as former chief shareholder Dietrich Mateschitz has sold his shares. Much of this shortfall is being made good by Mercedes, which paid for Räikkönen to be bought out of his contract, but a deal was done for a 63% stake in the team to be sold to sponsor Credit Suisse, so money won't be such a problem, enabling the team to test more in 2002.

A wise gamble

People said last year that Sauber was taking a huge gamble by employing Räikkönen straight from Formula Renault. In theory, it shouldn't have been allowed if the superlicence system had been adhered to, making him come via Formula 3000 or at

FOR THE RECORD

Country of origin	Switzerland
Team base	Hinwil, Switzerland
Website	www.sauber.ch
Active in Formula One	From 1993
Grands Prix contested	147
Wins	0
Pole positions	0
Fastest laps	0

DRIVERS + RESULTS 2001

Driver	Nationality	Races	Wins	Pts	Pos
Nick Heidfeld	German	17	-	12	7th
Kimi Räikkönen	Finnish	17	-	9	10th

CAR SPECIFICATIONS

Team principal	Peter Sauber
Technical director	Willy Rampf
Team manager	Beat Zehnder
Chief engineer	Jacky Eeckelaert
Test driver	None being used
Chassis	Sauber C21
Engine	Petronas Ferrari V10
Tyres	Bridgestone

through the season, rather than starting the season acceptably well and falling back as other teams went testing and made their cars work better. Rampf said that the C20 was a success as there had been a great focus on saving weight, allowing them to position ballast more than ever before. It also had new parts – often aerodynamic – for every race, and Rampf praised the technical feedback from Heidfeld in particular.

The drivers generally qualified at the tail of the top ten, mixing it with the Jordans and BARs, with Heidfeld's sixth place in qualifying at the A1-Ring ahead of both McLarens being something of a high point. It's just a shame that his launch control failed at the start, costing him 14 positions.

Both drivers were remarkably consistent in the first half of the year, with both producing drives that stand out. Heidfeld's best was when he kept his head to race to third in the wet-dry Brazilian GP, while the way in which Räikkönen kept up with the Ferraris at Imola until his steering wheel fell off was remarkable... It's not surprising that the FIA decided that evening that he'd passed his four-race probation with flying colours. Heidfeld went on to collect no fewer than five sixth-place finishes, while Räikkönen was fourth both at the A1-Ring and Montreal, then fifth at Silverstone.

From two seats to one

Sauber's background is sportscars rather than single-seaters, but helping Mercedes to win the Le Mans 24 Hours in 1989 earned the team its break with a semi-works engine in Formula One for 1993. They scored points on their debut, but a trio of third places for Heinz-Harald Frentzen and then two for Johnny Herbert were the highlights of their 1995, 1996 and 1997 seasons. In the last of these three years, Sauber started running ex-works Ferrari engines, a relationship that has continued to this day.

In a World of His Own: Peter Sauber savours a quiet moment

least through Formula Three. However, he proved a major talent, helped in no small part by the strength of the competitive package. With both Räikkönen and Heidfeld scoring points in the first round, things looked good for the Swiss team – certainly far better than they had in 2000 when Mika Salo and Pedro Diniz failed to shine.

Then, when Heidfeld raced to third place at Interlagos, people started to appreciate that Sauber had progressed, its engine proving more powerful than ever and its new chassis lighter and more aerodynamic than its predecessor the C20. Indeed, although the Petronas-badged 2000-specification Ferrari lagged behind the 2001 Ferrari, it was every bit the equal of rival engines from the likes of Mercedes and Cosworth, and even ahead of that of Honda.

This progress didn't come without a shock, however, as designer Sergio Rinland's departure in the run-up to the first round left Sauber seeking a replacement. McLaren's Stephen Taylor filled the vacancy. However, he returned to England "for personal reasons" a few months later, which shows how the Swiss team, based in Hinwil, struggles to keep personnel. Taylor ended up joining Jordan.

Willy Rampf assumed the helm of Sauber's design team, and for the first time in living memory the team carried on its development

NICK HEIDFELD

A POINT TO PROVE

There can be no greater incentive to attack than being passed over for your understudy, but this is precisely what happened to Nick Heidfeld last year when Kimi Räikkönen landed the much-prized second seat at McLaren.

Nationality	GERMAN
Born	MAY 10, 1977, MOENCHENGLADBACH, GERMANY
Website	www.nick-heidfeld.de
Teams	PROST 2000 SAUBER 2001–2002

CAREER RECORD

First Grand Prix	1999 AUSTRALIAN GP
Grand Prix starts	34
Grand Prix wins	0
best result: third, 2001 Brazilian GP	
Poles	0
Fastest laps	0
Points	12
Honours	1999 FORMULA 3000 CHAMPION, 1998 FORMULA 3000 RUNNER-UP, 1997 GERMAN FORMULA THREE CHAMPION, 1995 GERMAN FORMULA FORD RUNNER-UP, 1994 GERMAN FF1600 CHAMPION

100% Concentration: Heidfeld is a thinking driver

Little Nick Heidfeld looked crestfallen at last year's Italian GP when news broke that Mika Hakkinen was standing down from McLaren. Despite having been groomed since 1997 by Mercedes, been the team's test driver and driven as never before for Sauber, he'd been passed over for the vacancy. Worse than that, the place had been given to his junior team-mate Kimi Räikkönen, a driver whom he'd outqualified and outscored.

A shell-shocked Nick responded: "McLaren should know what they're doing, but I don't think I've done a lot wrong. I didn't do a worse job than him." Worse still, Nick feels that this year's Sauber has less chance of being as competitive as last year's, because many of the wealthier teams underperformed in 2001 and made Sauber look better than they were.

His move to Sauber from Prost for 2001 was a step up, but not one that people reckoned would give Nick the opportunity to show his skills. With a team-mate who was scarcely out of racing's kindergarten, he was going to be an undisputed number one, something that ought to have been supported by an excellent drive to fifth place in the season-opening Australian GP. A post-race penalty for Olivier Panis turned this into a career-best fourth place, but Räikkönen wasn't far behind, highlighting the fact that Nick was going to be kept on his toes through 2001.

After spinning out at Sepang, Nick really impressed with third place at Interlagos, albeit a lap down in an extraordinary wet/dry race. Outqualified by Räikkönen for the first time at Imola, Nick then ran without drama – or his team-mate's pace – through to seventh. At least the Spanish GP produced a score, but then Nick achieved another milestone when he qualified sixth in Austria. Sadly, he stalled on the grid and kissed goodbye to a run in the points. With all but the drivers for the top three teams struggling to get into the points, Nick did well to claim four more sixth place finishes by the season's end, but the fact that Kimi collected two fourths and a fifth might have said something too, although Nick had the upper hand as the season came to a close.

A golden past

If Nick had been judged on his first year in Formula One, in 2000, people might say that he didn't shine. But that was for a faltering Prost team, for whom even illustrious team-mate Jean Alesi failed to score. Yet there are many people in Formula One who continue to consider form in terms of what drivers have achieved in the past few races, never considering a driver's career before they "miraculously" appeared in Formula One.

Nick was a hotshot in karts, impressed in Formula Ford, then won the German Formula Three crown in 1997. He very nearly added the Formula 3000 title in 1998, but was pipped to the post by Juan Pablo Montoya. However, Nick made amends in 1999.

FELIPE MASSA

ANOTHER KIMI RÄIKKÖNEN?

Sauber is taking a punt for the second year in a row, hoping to bring a talented newcomer into Formula One early in the hope of landing a future champion. After Kimi Räikkönen, Felipe Massa may prove that lightning can strike twice.

CAREER RECORD

First Grand Prix	2002
	AUSTRALIAN GP
Grand Prix starts	0
Grand Prix wins	0
Poles	0
Fastest laps	0
Points	0
Honours	2001 EUROPEAN
	FORMULA 3000 CHAMPION,
	2000 EUROPEAN & ITALIAN
	FORMULA RENAULT CHAMPION,
	1999 BRAZILIAN FORMULA
	CHEVROLET CHAMPION

After news broke that it was losing Kimi Räikkönen just one year into a three-year contract, it took Sauber only a few weeks to announce that it was going for another rookie to replace him. And not just a rookie from Formula One's feeder formula, the FIA International Formula 3000 series, but from the second-division Euro series based largely in Italy. However, Felipe Massa is clearly no mug behind the wheel.

Much as Räikkönen convinced Sauber of his ability in a series of tests at the end of 2000, Felipe did the same last autumn at Mugello. Race engineer Jacky Eeckelaert – a former racer himself – is credited with spotting the great ahead of the good, and he was sure after watching Felipe's second test run at the Ferrari-owned Magello circuit that the young Brazilian has what it takes. After all, he'd just eclipsed Michael Schumacher's best time around the circuit... Technical director Willy Rampf was impressed too: "It was a pleasure to work with him. He was very focused."

Team boss Peter Sauber explained his faith in Felipe: "By deciding on Felipe, we've once again opted for a talented young driver. He convinced us with his excellent performance during tests at Mugello, where he demonstrated his promising potential in a remarkable manner."

Felipe appears to be a driver who isn't fazed by much. Only time will tell if this will stand true for the rigours of Formula One, in which there's more to life than just driving a car quickly in tests. Racing is an entirely different proposition, and then there's the massive out-of-car pressure from sponsors and the media. Add to this the fact that this year's Sauber isn't expected to be as competitive as last year's car, and perhaps Felipe will struggle to make the impression that Räikkönen did. However, much to the chagrin of the Formula 3000 frontrunners past whom he has leaped, Felipe appears to be the "real thing".

Face of the Future: Felipe was little known in 2001. Now he must deliver in the big time

A brief apprenticeship

Anyone who makes it to Formula One by the age of 20 can't have had a lengthy run through the junior formulae, but Felipe made such good progress in each of the three formulae in which he has raced that it makes perfect sense. His first year in cars yielded the Brazilian Formula Chevrolet title. He came to Europe in 2000 and went so well in Italian Formula Renault that his team scrimped to enter him in European Championship rounds. Felipe won these too, and went on to become champion in both series. In addition to his Formula 3000 campaign that he won with six wins from eight starts for the Draco Racing team, Felipe also raced for Alfa Romeo, being seconded to support Fabrizio Giovanardi's championship challenge in the European Touring Car Championship. He impressed, too, showing an ability to adapt instantly to another form of competition machinery.

JORDAN

TIME TO DELIVER

The pressure was on last year as Jordan attempted to prove that all it needed to succeed was a strong works engine, but Honda didn't really deliver and the results weren't all that Eddie Jordan had hoped.

Jordan's decision to sign Takuma Sato – the 24-year-old Japanese driver who dominated British Formula 3 last year – to fill its second seat set tongues wagging. Many said this was done only as a means of ensuring a continuation of the team's Honda engine supply in 2004 and beyond. However, Eddie Jordan is adamant that he simply wants to chance his arm with a young driver again, rather than being disappointed by an older star, as he was by Damon Hill in 1999 and by Heinz-Harald Frentzen in 2001.

With Sato being joined by former Jordan driver Giancarlo Fisichella, the Irishman will hope that the Italian's experience can be used to good effect to add to Sato's speed.

Team Talk: Eddie Jordan and Jordan's commercial director Ian Phillips compare notes and catch up on the news

He'll also be hoping that the poor reliability that blighted Jarno Trulli in particular last year can be sorted. A whole dollop more power from Honda would be appreciated, too, as the Japanese engine wasn't the team's strongest ingredient last year.

This year will be Eghbal Hamidy's first chance to pen a car for Jordan, so the drivers will be hoping he produces one as sleek as the cars he used to design for Arrows. He is to be supported by former Jordan design chief Gary Anderson.

A year that slipped away

Before Williams got up to speed, Jordan's drivers looked as though they might be able to propel the team back to third place behind Ferrari and McLaren in the constructors' rankings. In Melbourne, Frentzen came fifth despite being tipped into a spin. Then Trulli led in the downpour at Sepang, but damaged his car by spinning, while Frentzen worked his way up the order to fourth. Frentzen was heading for third at Interlagos until his engine cut in the closing laps, but at least Trulli scored in fifth. Trulli then ran third for the first segment of the San Marino GP after a good start, but he then slipped to fifth. However, this was the race in which Williams found its feet, and Jordan's drivers found it very hard to score points hereafter.

The dangers of launch control systems not working was made plain at the Spanish GP, as Frentzen sat stationary on the grid while those behind him somehow squeezed past. At least Trulli benefited from the race's retirements to finish fourth. That was nothing compared with what happened at the

A1-Ring, however, when both drivers were stranded on the grid.

In the run-up to the Canadian GP, the tension in the camp was severe, as Honda was expected to decide which of Jordan and BAR it was going to drop for 2002 in its quest to achieve greater competitiveness. However, to the relief of both Jordan and BAR, Honda elected to continue to supply both of them. Perhaps of greater concern was the fact that Honda appeared to make no progress as rival engine manufacturers found more horsepower, with rumours circulating that every extra horsepower was costing millions.

A headache from crashing at Monaco caused Frentzen to miss the Canadian GP after he exacerbated it further by also crashing in practice. Test driver Ricardo Zonta stepped up and finished seventh. The run of races that followed yielded next to no points with the cars tending to drop away, failing to use their tyres well as they wore, and it all came to a head with the sacking of Frentzen in the run-up to his home race at Hockenheim. It wasn't a weekend that Jordan will want to remember, as just about everything that could go wrong on the track

THE VIPS

EDDIE JORDAN
Snappy one-liners may be his trademark, but this often-flamboyant Irishman has a steely determination, something that has been obvious from the moment that he turned his back on his own racing career to manage title-winning teams in Formula Three and Formula 3000 before reaching Formula One in 1991. His team won grands prix in 1998 and 1999.

EGHBAL HAMIDY
This aeronautical engineer from Iran got his first taste of Formula One with Williams. An eight-year spell there was followed by a move to Stewart for their first season in 1997. Arrows was his next port of call before joining Jordan at the end of 2000 as technical director.

did – proving that the Germans really did invent *Schadenfreude*. Zonta filled the gap, but he was replaced by Jean Alesi for the rest of the year thanks to his long-standing connections with Eddie Jordan. Of Frentzen's departure we heard little, as the details were *sub judice*, but it was thought that he'd attended a Toyota test – a near-heretical act for a Honda driver.

Hereafter, Trulli was robbed frequently when set for points, but Alesi scored on his second outing for the team, in Belgium. This came his way, though, only as Trulli retired from fifth place several laps from home. Then Trulli was hit at the first corner of the Italian GP after qualifying fifth, but he gave Jordan a boost by finishing fourth at Indianapolis, with Alesi seventh. However, the plank under Trulli's car was found to be illegal. Jordan was fortunate to have him reinstated on a technicality at the subsequent appeal, and this elevated him from ninth in the rankings to seventh, also lifting Jordan from equal fifth with BAR to fifth on its own – a difference worth several million pounds.

From racer to boss

A racer himself, Eddie Jordan decided he didn't have the skill to go all the way so turned to team management. His Formula Three team won the British crown with Johnny Herbert in 1987, then stepped up to Formula 3000 and took that title with Jean Alesi in 1989. Jordan made the leap into Formula One in 1991 and, amazingly, ranked fifth overall. A wrong engine choice tripped them up, but Jordan started to shine again and put Rubens Barrichello and Eddie Irvine on the podium at the 1995 Canadian GP. Fisichella and Ralf Schumacher starred for Jordan in 1997, but the team's breakthrough came in 1998 when Damon Hill led Ralf home for a one-two in the Belgian GP. Frentzen won twice in 1999, helping Jordan to rank third overall.

Fluctuating Form: There were times last year when Jordan could keep ahead of McLaren, but not many... This is in the early laps in Spain

FOR THE RECORD

Country of origin	**England**
Team base	**Silverstone, England**
Website	**www.f1jordan.com**
Active in Formula One	**From 1991**
Grands Prix contested	**80**
Wins	**3**
Pole positions	**2**
Fastest laps	**2**

DRIVERS + RESULTS 2001

Driver	Nationality	Races	Wins	Pts	Pos
Jean Alesi *	French	5	-	5	14th
Heinz-Harald Frentzen	German	10	-	6	12th
Jarno Trulli	Italian	17	-	12	7th
Ricardo Zonta	Brazilian	2	-	-	-

* Four of Alesi's points were scored when he drove for Prost

CAR SPECIFICATIONS

Team principal	**Eddie Jordan**
Team manager	**Trevor Foster**
Chief designer	**Eghbal Hamidy**
Chief engineer	**David Brown**
Test driver	**Ryo Fukuda**
Chassis	**Jordan EJ12**
Engine	**Honda V10**
Tyres	**Bridgestone**

GIANCARLO FISICHELLA

BACK TO JORDAN

Giancarlo Fisichella could be looking ruefully across at Renault Sport this year, as the team that he helped bring towards competitiveness last year could be set to bloom and outpace his new team, Jordan.

There are 17 races ahead to discover whether Giancarlo or his fellow Flavio Briatore-managed driver Jarno Trulli has got the better of their close-season swap, with Giancarlo having gone from Benetton (now Renault Sport) to Jordan and Trulli moving in the opposite direction.

Giancarlo has thus been reunited with Eddie Jordan, who converted him into a frontrunner in 1997 and didn't want to see him go, so they ought to get on. However, people are saying that the nationality of team-mate Takuma Sato could count against Giancarlo as Jordan's engines come from Japanese manufacturer Honda. Giancarlo has dismissed this assessment: "I've always been faster than my team-mates. It'll be part of my job to help him, but I'm competing against him as much as anyone else."

One of the best-paid drivers in Formula One, Giancarlo appeared to be one with more than his reputation to lose in 2001, as he'd been criticised by Briatore for not using his head in 2000, and he was being joined by 2000's rookie star Jenson Button. With the Benetton-Renault combination proving a bit weak, he and Button struggled to outqualify even the Minardis. However, Giancarlo made a better fist of it than Button, and his drive to sixth in Brazil was one of the year's top drives – albeit one noticed only by the most perceptive of observers. He'd clearly raised his game, but this must have been hard to manage when his car was at its worst in the first half of the season.

Commendably, Giancarlo persevered, but that sixth at Interlagos was his only top-10 finish in the first 11 races. Then, as Renault unleashed more horsepower and Mike Gascoyne got on top of the aerodynamics of the car that he'd inherited, results arrived,

Thoughtful: Giancarlo's move back to Jordan may not prove inspired if Renault shines

with fourth in the German GP followed by running second and finishing third in the Belgian GP. Suddenly, people started talking of Giancarlo again.

Destined for the top

A glance at Giancarlo's CV is enough to identify that he was a driver who had the attributes to reach Formula One. After being one of the leading drivers in European karting, he moved to cars in Italy's Formula Alfa Boxer series in 1991. Giancarlo was a winner by the end of his first season in Italian Formula Three and runner-up overall in his second. Not only did he win the title in 1994, but he also won the race supporting the

Monaco GP. Without the finance to do Formula 3000, Giancarlo raced for Alfa Romeo in the International Touring Car Championship, in which he shone. In the second of these seasons, 1996, he made it to Formula One with Minardi. Jordan signed him for 1997, with Giancarlo leading the German GP before peaking with second in the Belgian GP. Briatore had him under contract, though, and took him to Benetton for 1998, where he stayed until last year, claiming four more second places.

TAKUMA SATO

JAPAN'S RISING SON

Japanese Formula One fans have been praying for a star of their own and many believe that at last, in new Jordan signing Takuma Sato, they might have found one.

New Partnership: Eddie Jordan and British Formula Three champion Takuma Sato are all smiles at the announcement of the team's new number two at the Japanese Grand Prix last October

Nationality	JAPANESE
Born	JANUARY 28, 1977, TOKYO, JAPAN
Website	www.takumasato.com
Teams	JORDAN 2002

CAREER RECORD

First Grand Prix	2002 AUSTRALIAN GP
Grand Prix starts	0
Grand Prix wins	0
Poles	0
Fastest laps	0
Points	0
Honours	2001 BRITISH FORMULA THREE CHAMPION

Apart from Takuma Sato himself, no one will be more delighted than Formula One supremo Bernie Ecclestone if Japan's latest Formula One hope can become a regular point scorer or even – dare one say it – race winner. You see, Japan is aching for a driver of their own to do well on the sport's biggest stage. Indeed, after years of underachievement from Japanese drivers – with Aguri Suzuki's third position in the 1990 Japanese GP their only podium result – it's essential that one of their own succeeds or their fans could lose interest.

Examining the many successes of Takuma's racing career, you can see why Eddie Jordan would have been keen to sign him to partner Giancarlo Fisichella – especially now that the trend for spotting a driver and snapping them up on to long-term contracts before they have even shown their hand in Formula 3000 is all the rage. However, the fact that Takuma is Japanese and so is Honda, Jordan's engine supplier, won't have escaped anyone's notice.

That said, Takuma is the most talented Japanese driver to have made it to Formula One and, with excellent linguistic skills, is sure not to suffer the same pitfalls that wiped out the promising career of the last Japanese hotshot, Toranosuke Takagi, several years ago.

On top of this, Takuma already has a year's experience of the folk at Jordan, having been the team's test driver through last year, so neither the car nor the personnel ought to spring any surprises.

A European training

Unlike the vast majority of drivers in Formula One, Takuma wasn't pushed into the sport for a parent's vicarious thrills. Indeed, he only started in karts when he was 19. That he hadn't spent his teenage years racing makes his progress all the more remarkable.

Winning a racing scholarship at Suzuka in 1997 launched him into car racing but, now with parental support, Takuma elected to head immediately to Europe, racing in 1998 in Formula Vauxhall Junior – managed by Diamond Racing, the team that ran Mika Hakkinen in the junior categories.

He advanced to Formula Vauxhall in 1999 and became a race winner in the British and European series. Graduating to Formula Three in 2000, Takuma won four races to rank third overall. Staying on for last season, Takuma was one of the pre-season favourites and didn't disappoint, storming to an impressive tally of 12 wins for Carlin Motorsport. He also won the invitation race at Zandvoort and a support race for the British GP at Silverstone. Rivals hinted that Takuma's Mugen Honda engines were perhaps more special than most, but that's sour grapes for you...

Showing how Japan's young drivers are finally on the charge, Takuma's success in winning the British crown was added to by compatriots Ryo Fukuda and Toshihiro Kaneishi winning the French and German Formula Three titles respectively.

BAR

BAR got serious last December when a palace coup resulted in the management replacing founder Craig Pollock with David Richards. Drivers Olivier Panis and Jacques Villeneuve have kept their jobs.

Same Again: BAR is sticking with its closely-matched 2001 pairing of Jacques Villeneuve and Olivier Panis for the 2002 World Championship, but the management has changed somewhat...

British American Racing had a shake-up before Christmas when team principal Craig Pollock parted company with the team after a move from within headed by BAR chairman Ken Clarke. Yes, the man who founded BAR was out, with rally chief and one-time Benetton boss David Richards taking over at the helm. Lead driver Jacques Villeneuve – a long-time friend of Pollock's – wasn't impressed and it will be interesting to see how he responds to his new team boss.

Looking at the ingredients, drivers Villeneuve and Olivier Panis have the same chance as Jordan's drivers in terms of power, as both teams are powered by Honda, albeit with BAR strengthening its link by extending its deal with Honda until the end of 2004 and Richards's Prodrive engineering company starting a technical relationship with Honda. Both teams are also using Bridgestone tyres.

But what will separate them will be the quality of their chassis. On the evidence of last year, Jordan's drivers probably have rather more reason to smile, as the new BAR 004 chassis comes from the same pen as last year's: Malcolm Oastler's.

BAR acknowledged that the 2001 chassis was no gem. Indeed, Villeneuve realised as much after his first test in the car. So, to this end, engineering director Oastler has been bolstered by the arrival of aerodynamicist Geoff Willis from Williams. This won't help with the creation of 004, as he's contracted to Williams until the start of March, but at least he'll be able to help develop the car through the season. However, Mark Bowen has joined from Ferrari to take charge of the design of 004's mechanical parts.

"I've been conscious for some time," said Oastler, "that the job I've been trying to do is too much for one person. At the same time, we've been missing the senior technical experience that can only come from the teams at the top."

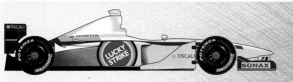

Country of origin	England
Team base	Brackley, England
Website	www.britishamericanracing.com
Active in Formula One	From 1999
Grands Prix contested	50
Wins	0
Pole positions	0
Fastest laps	0

DRIVERS + RESULTS 2001

Driver	Nationality	Races	Wins	Pts	Pos
Olivier Panis	French	17	-	5	14th
Jacques Villeneuve	Canadian	17	-	12	7th

CAR SPECIFICATIONS

Team principal	David Richards
Engineering director	Malcolm Oastler
Technical director	Geoff Willis
Team manager	Ron Meadows
Chief engineer	James Robinson
Test drivers	Anthony Davidson & Darren Manning
Chassis	BAR 004
Engine	Honda V10
Tyres	Bridgestone

Good in parts

BAR prayed that 2001 was going to prove to be a case of third time lucky after a weaker-than-hoped-for first two seasons. This was to be the team's big year, with works Honda engines offering the opportunity to see how they compared firstly with Jordan and secondly with their other rivals. However, the early races showed that Jordan still had the upper hand, although Panis would have scored first time out but for an alleged yellow-flag infringement that dropped him from fourth to seventh. But, after Panis grabbed a lapped fourth in the Brazilian GP, Villeneuve went one better in the Spanish GP to gave BAR its first podium position, finishing third. This was something of a lucky result, but the team was only too happy to make the most of this fillip to its spirits.

With a clutch more points following in the next two races, things were looking good, especially as Villeneuve was clearly being kept on his toes as never before by the challenge from within from Panis, who looked the sharper of the two over the first six races. Not always on the bubble in qualifying, Villeneuve normally stepped up a gear in the races themselves. This was good for BAR, as it made it a proper two-car team for the first time. Then, on the eve of the Austrian GP, Villeneuve admitted that he'd been suffering from a displaced disc in his spine sustained in his accident with Ralf Schumacher in the Australian GP that left a marshal dead. Not surprisingly, in having to nurse this problem, he wasn't as positive over the kerbs as he would have liked...

But then the wheels came off the bus until Villeneuve produced an inspired race in the German GP, using a one-stop strategy to climb from twelfth to an eventual third.

With points becoming ever harder to come by – especially as Williams got its reliability problems sorted – BAR was frustrated when Jordan won its appeal on a technicality against Trulli's disqualification in the United States GP, as the three points that Trulli regained were sufficient to drop BAR from its position of sharing fifth place in the constructors' championship, costing them millions.

In with a whimper

BAR arrived with a bang in 1998, with co-founder Adrian Reynard predicting that they would win on their debut, as his Reynard cars had in Formula Ford, Formula Three, Formula 3000 and then in Indycars. His partner, Craig Pollock, tried to underplay this bravado, saying that the team *would* win but more likely at the end of the season. However, many were already laughing at BAR's launch catchline of "a tradition of excellence" – this from a team that had never raced before, having been created specifically to race in Formula One. Villeneuve and his rookie team-mate Ricardo Zonta failed to finish race after race, with team leader Villeneuve's first finish coming in the twelfth round. Neither even managed to score a point, with stand-in Mika Salo's seventh place in the Spanish GP the team's best result. So, sights were set lower for 2000 and matters went considerably better, with both drivers finishing in the points in the opening race. More followed, with Villeneuve finishing fourth four times to help BAR to rank fifth.

Mr Motivator: David Richards has been brought in to replace Craig Pollock

JACQUES VILLENEUVE

NOW OR NEVER

This was always going to be a crunch season for Jacques Villeneuve at BAR. Yet, with his team-founding friend Craig Pollock having been forced out, he may be looking elsewhere for a drive in 2003.

Jacques is a driver who loves to push his car to the limit and to race hard but fair. This was clear when he was the lone driver to stand up to Michael Schumacher's race-morning request at last year's Italian GP (in the wake of the World Trade Center disaster) not to overtake into the first two chicanes in the interest of safety. Respect for this purist reached an even higher level.

However, Jacques is also paying for his ideals as he faces a fourth year with BAR, the team he co-founded with Craig Pollock rather than stay with a top team. Back in 1999 he felt that political infighting was destabilising their progress. At the start of 2001, he criticised their latest chassis. By the end of the year, he started to accept that perhaps his chance to race for a top team again had gone forever. With no car, engine or tyre ingredients changing for 2002, he's unlikely to win in 2002. But, with Pollock gone, he may not even stay to the end of the year.

Jacques didn't have the best start to last year's world championship when he struck Ralf Schumacher's Williams in the Australian GP, with one of his wheels killing a marshal. Jacques appeared shaken emotionally rather than physically, but later in the year admitted that he still had back pain.

Jacques raced well in Spain, but even he couldn't have predicted that the loss of most of the top drivers through the race would enable him to take third place. The honeymoon period was short, though, as he was out of the points in Austria, but he bounced back to fourth at Monaco. With the exception of the German GP, in which he finished third, the year was a disappointment – one in which he was always kept honest by team-mate Olivier Panis.

Happy: Jacques Villeneuve was a lucky third in Spain

Famous son of a famous father

It was inevitable that Jacques would be compared to his late, great father Gilles when he began racing at the age of 18, but he let it be known that he was his own man. Speed came with experience in Italian Formula Three. A spell in Japanese Formula Three left him runner-up, but he also met up with his former teacher Pollock who agreed to manage his career. Pollock guided Jacques to the USA, where he impressed in Formula Atlantic in 1993. Jacques stepped up to Indycars and followed the rookie-of-the-year title in 1994 by winning the title itself in 1995. And then his passage to Formula One was eased by Bernie Ecclestone, with Jacques joining Williams for 1996. The team was dominant and Jacques won four times to be runner-up to team-mate Damon Hill. Team leader in 1997, the title was his but, after a poor year in 1998 with non-works engines, Jacques rejoined Pollock for the formation of BAR, for whom four fourth places in 2000 were the highlights of his first two seasons with the team.

TRACK NOTES

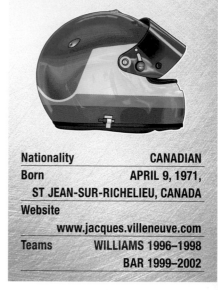

Nationality	CANADIAN
Born	APRIL 9, 1971,
	ST JEAN-SUR-RICHELIEU, CANADA
Website	
	www.jacques.villeneuve.com
Teams	WILLIAMS 1996–1998
	BAR 1999–2002

CAREER RECORD

First Grand Prix	1996
	AUSTRALIAN GP
Grand Prix starts	99
Grand Prix wins	11
	1996 European GP, British GP
	Hungarian GP, Portuguese GP,
	1997 Brazilian GP, Argentinian GP,
	Spanish GP, British GP,
	Hungarian GP, Austrian GP,
	Luxembourg GP
Poles	13
Fastest laps	9
Points	209
Honours	1997 FORMULA ONE
	CHAMPION,
	1996 FORMULA ONE RUNNER-UP,
	1995 INDYCAR CHAMPION &
	INDY 500 WINNER,
	1994 INDYCAR ROOKIE OF THE YEAR,
	1993 TOYOTA ATLANTIC
	ROOKIE OF THE YEAR,
	1992 JAPANESE FORMULA
	THREE RUNNER-UP

OLIVIER PANIS

A POINT TO PROVE

Olivier Panis worked extremely hard for little reward last year – in terms of points, that is – so rest assured that the veteran Frenchman will be out to make amends in this, his second year with BAR.

TRACK NOTES

Nationality	FRENCH
Born	SEPTEMBER 2, 1966, LYONS, FRANCE
Website	www.olivier-panis.com
Teams	LIGIER/PROST 1994–1999, BAR 2001–2002

CAREER RECORD

First Grand Prix	1994
	BRAZILIAN GP
Grand Prix starts	108
Grand Prix wins	1
	1996 Monaco GP
Poles	0
Fastest laps	0
Points	61
Honours	1993 FORMULA 3000 CHAMPION, 1991 FRENCH FORMULA THREE RUNNER-UP, 1989 FRENCH FORMULA RENAULT CHAMPION

Last Chance Saloon: Olivier knows he needs a good year to keep him in the frame

Olivier is the sort of driver that you want on board if you're attempting to take your team forward, for this charming Frenchman is fast, intelligent, consistent and, by all accounts, an analytical developer of a car. Yet, after 108 grands prix, he has won just one. But still the fire burns.

His testing times through 2000 for McLaren suggested that he wasn't the washed-up driver that he had seemed to be when racing for Prost through 1998 and 1999. Indeed, he often matched the pace of Mika Hakkinen and David Coulthard. But it was only once Olivier returned to the big stage and started racing again for BAR last season that people were really able to judge the extent of Olivier's rehabilitation. And his sparkling form was enough to help drivers-turned-test-drivers like Alexander Wurz not to give up hope of ever making a return to the main stage.

Measured against his team-mate Jacques Villeneuve – the driver around whom the team had been built – Olivier came out very well. Indeed, he was often faster than the French–Canadian in practice and was his equal in qualifying over the first six races. Although they're good friends, this started to rattle Jacques, especially as he noticed how popular Olivier was becoming within the team.

Olivier was also the first of the duo to be in the points. This should have been at the Australian GP, but a time penalty for allegedly passing under yellow flags dropped him from fourth to seventh. However, Olivier did claim fourth when he hunted down Jordan's Jarno Trulli at Interlagos and fifth at the A1-Ring. But, such was the dropaway in BAR's relative competitiveness that Olivier never scored again in the remaining 11 grands prix.

A biennial winner

There was a definite pattern to Olivier's passage through the junior single-seater categories. It was a case of one year on, one year off as he grabbed the French Formula Renault title in his second year of car racing in 1989. Moving up to French Formula Three, he won that at his second attempt in 1991. Then, like clockwork, he took two years to land the Formula 3000 title. But then came Formula One, starting with Ligier in 1994, when he earned praise for not only outscoring team-mate Eric Bernard, but also for finishing every race but one. After a shock second-place finish in the 1995 Australian GP, he pulled out a single stunning race in 1996, winning in the wet at Monaco. The 1997 season was full of promise as he flew on the new Bridgestone tyres, claiming a second, a third and a fourth before breaking both legs in Montreal. Back before the year was out, Olivier found the next two years a struggle as the team became Prost. And so Olivier found himself as a test driver in 2000. Luckily, this was with McLaren.

RENAULT SPORT

BACK IN YELLOW

Benetton is no more. Long live Renault Sport. And now that its radical, wide-angle V10 has been developed through last year with Benetton, the team could be looking at win races on its return.

Contemplation: Mike Gascoyne and team chief Flavio Briatore ponder one of the problems that confronted them in 2001

N o longer will the cars run by Flavio Briatore's team be pale blue, and no longer will they be Benettons. Instead, from this year onward they will be Renault Sports, and will be turned out in Renault's traditional yellow, black and white colours. Apart from the change of name and livery, little will be different. But all the signs are that the results will be, and they're expected to be a considerable improvement on those achieved by a team that struggled before finding its way late in the 2000–2001 season.

This year's B202 will be the first car in which Gascoyne has been involved from the outset, as he inherited the B201 after joining from Jordan and spent as much time sorting out Benetton's technical facilities as he did developing the car. So, expect the B202 to be a more cohesive package.

Renault's 111-degree V10 engine appeared to be going nowhere last year, often even constituting an embarrassment in the first half of the year. But Renault's record in building the ultimate in engines is second to none since the 1980s, and it duly started to advance; so, again, expect it to be right at the front in the horsepower stakes – just as BMW's was in 2001 in the German marque's second year back in Formula One.

Jenson Button stays on for a second year with the team after patching up his differences with Briatore. The other seat is to be occupied by Jarno Trulli after a swap with fellow Italian and fellow Briatore-managed driver Giancarlo Fisichella, who has moved in the opposite direction to Jordan. This looks to be a potent driving line-up, with Button likely to return to the confident form that marked him out as such a star in his maiden Formula One season with Williams in 2000.

A slow start

Wins were never in the offing last year. In fact, Benetton had never looked as woeful as they did at the start of last season. In 1995, the team won the constructors' championship, yet here they were scrapping with Minardi at the tail of the field. Button sometimes didn't go out in practice as the team was saving engine life... And all the team could say was that it was waiting for the next evolution of Renault's radical engine that was arriving at the French GP. When Gascoyne failed to attend the Austrian GP, rumours started to abound that a scapegoat was being found, but Benetton said that he was concentrating instead on development parts. And, boy, did the team need them as its engine was said to

THE VIPS

FLAVIO BRIATORE
Even now, Briatore claims not to care much for Formula One, but this former high-flier in the Benetton knitwear empire has been at the sharp end since he took the reins of Benetton's Formula One team in 1989. Alongside this, he set up Supertec to supply ex-works Renault engines in 1998. The chain-smoking Italian also has a host of drivers on his books.

PAT SYMONDS
A racing-car designer since 1976, Pat is a backbone of the team, having been with Toleman before it became Benetton in 1986 and now as Renault Sport. As Executive Director of Engineering, Pat not only guides the team's technical direction but also calls many of the shots on the pitwall.

be giving away up to 100bhp to Williams' mighty BMW powerplants units.

Many said, though, that the team's lack of speed was proof that not all the blame should lie with Renault for its underperforming engine, and that the B201 chassis wasn't all that it should be, because although it looked to have acceptable downforce and mechanical grip, its aerodynamic efficiency was unacceptable.

The only highlight of the first six races was that Fisichella salvaged a point by staying around to the end of the Brazilian GP. Indeed, the Italian was driving as well as ever, if not better, having been stimulated by the arrival of Button – the hotshot of 2000. Ironically, it was Button who had the superior finishing record when the team was at its lowest ebb, being classified in five of the first six races, albeit never higher than 10th.

The French GP marked the first upgrade of Renault's V10, but the leap ahead in power must have been small at this stage as they still only qualified 16th and 17th. Briatore even tendered his resignation, but Renault wouldn't accept it. On top of that, people started linking Gascoyne to a move to Minardi as he'd been seen talking to team boss Paul Stoddart on the grid...

The atmosphere was still tense, but a new aerodynamic package for the German GP yielded dividends, with Fisichella and Button not only finishing on the same lap as the race winner, but doing so in fourth and fifth places. Further aerodynamic changes came good at the Belgian GP, alleviating the pressure on Gascoyne to turn the team around when Fisichella ran second for much of the race before being eased back to third by McLaren's David Coulthard. Twenty-four-hour shifts spent honing their aerodynamic package in their wind tunnel had worked. And a series of steps forward from Renault.

Benetton finished just out of the points in the final three grands prix, but the omens were starting to look hugely better for 2002.

A double past

To examine the history of this year's Renault Sport team, one needs to consider the pasts of both Benetton and Renault. Benetton was spawned from the Toleman team in 1986, started winning races at the end of that year, then guided Michael Schumacher to the drivers' title in 1994 and 1995, winning the constructors' championship for the one and only time in the second of these years. Renault arrived in 1977, as the first team to enter a turbocharged car, with its first win coming in 1979. Its best hope of a world title came in 1981 when Alain Prost was pipped by Nelson Piquet, then Renault shut-up shop at the end of 1985, concentrating thereafter on providing title-winning engines for Williams from 1989 to 1997.

Power Pow-Wow: Mike Gascoyne talks technical talk on the pit wall

Country of origin	England
Team base	Enstone, England
Website	www.renaultf1.com
Active in Formula One	From 1986 (as Benetton)
Grands Prix contested	361
Wins	27
Pole positions	16
Fastest laps	35

DRIVERS + RESULTS 2001

Driver	Nationality	Races	Wins	Pts	Pos
Jenson Button	English	17	-	2	17th
Giancarlo Fisichella	Italian	17	-	8	11th

CAR SPECIFICATIONS

Team principal	Flavio Briatore
Technical director	Mike Gascoyne
Team manager	Steve Nielsen
Chief designer	Tim Densham
Chief engineer	Pat Symonds
Test driver	Fernando Alonso
Chassis	Renault R202
Engine	Renault V10
Tyres	Michelin

JARNO TRULLI

A GOOD MOVE MADE

Transferring across from Jordan to the newly-renamed Renault Sport team could be just the move needed to convert Jarno Trulli from a driver with potential galore into a grand prix winner.

Some say that the swapping of Jarno Trulli and Giancarlo Fisichella between Jordan and Renault Sport for 2002 is down to the fact that Flavio Briatore, manager of both drivers, wanted to shift the driver on a larger retainer (Fisichella) out of his team to keep the bills down. However, much as Fisichella restored his reputation last year, Jarno Trulli looks to be the more likely champion given the right equipment. Yet there are some who talk of him as being a qualifier rather than a racer. Closer analysis of his record for 2001 reveals that he was frequently robbed when set for points. Such was the bad luck that dogged Jarno that he said mid-season: "Every weekend I try to forget what went before and hope that it's going to be alright." Sadly, time after time, it wasn't.

Easily the best of the Jordan drivers last year, expect Jarno to shine for Renault Sport, as Renault's second-generation engine is sure to pack a punch in the back of a Mike

Looking Ahead: What chance Trulli is looking at his maiden grand prix victory with Renault?

Gascoyne-designed car. There is, of course, the matter of being partnered with Jenson Button, as they seemed to have an irresistible attraction to each other at the end of last year, but they should be fine together.

A misfire ruined a likely run to fourth place in Australia, then Jarno led at Sepang, but spun off within a lap of the rain arriving. In Brazil, Jordan called Jarno in for his pit-stop moments before rain fell. He was then given wets at a second pit-stop when intermediates were what was needed, and he was lucky to finish fifth.

A flying start helped Jarno leap from fifth to third at Imola, but he couldn't keep with the pace and fell to fifth. Fourth in the Spanish GP suggests an improvement in form, yet in reality it was largely down to the failure of others. However, no points went begging more painfully than his run in the Belgian GP that had him set for fifth until his engine blew. Then, no sooner had Jarno finished fourth in the US GP than he was disqualified for an irregularity to his car's plank. He was later reinstated after Jordan won an appeal.

TRACK NOTES

Nationality	ITALIAN
Born	JULY 13, 1974, PESCARA, ITALY
Website	www.jarnotrulli.com
Teams	MINARDI 1997
	PROST 1997–1999
	JORDAN 2000–2001
	RENAULT 2002

CAREER RECORD

First Grand Prix	1997
	AUSTRALIAN GP
Grand Prix starts	80
Grand Prix wins	0
best result: second 1999 European GP	
Poles	0
Fastest laps	0
Points	29
Honours	1996 GERMAN
	FORMULA THREE CHAMPION,
	1994 WORLD KART CHAMPION

The first of a kind

Jarno was the first of the new breed of drivers who leap almost straight from karts to Formula One. Jarno jumped from being karting world champion to Formula Three midway through 1995, propelled into the German series by Briatore. A winner before the year was out, he won the title in 1996 and skipped straight on to Formula One in 1997, bucking the trend of going via Formula 3000. He learned his craft with Minardi, then subbed for Olivier Panis at Prost, even leading the first half of the Austrian GP. His next two seasons were masked by Prost's poor form, with second in the 1999 European GP a rare highlight. In 2000, Jarno shone with Jordan, qualifying on the front row at Monaco and again at Spa-Francorchamps.

JENSON BUTTON

Lauded for his natural skills after his first year of Formula One in 2000, Jenson Button saw the flip side of the coin last year, as he struggled with a somewhat uncompetitive Benetton. Perversely, the experience could have been his making.

TRACK NOTES

Nationality	ENGLISH
Born	JANUARY 19, 1980, FROME, ENGLAND
Website	www.jensonbutton.co.uk
Teams	WILLIAMS 2000 BENETTON/RENAULT 2001–2002

CAREER RECORD

First Grand Prix	2000 AUSTRALIAN GP
Grand Prix starts	34
Grand Prix wins	0
best result: fourth, 2000 German GP	
Poles	0
Fastest laps	0
Points	14
Honours	1999 MACAU FORMULA THREE RUNNER-UP, 1998 FORMULA FORD FESTIVAL WINNER & BRITISH FORMULA FORD CHAMPION, 1998 McLAREN AUTOSPORT BRDC YOUNG DRIVER, 1997 EUROPEAN SUPER A KART CHAMPION, 1991 BRITISH CADET KART CHAMPION

Serious Business: Jenson Button knows that he must harness his ability to the full to shine again in 2002 to keep his name up in lights

Jenson must wonder what happened in the year that followed his startling Formula One debut for Williams, for the 2001 season with Benetton was an uphill struggle. Then, as the drivers left for their winter break, Eddie Irvine described him as "the weakest link".

Although it was clear that the Renault-powered Benetton was disappointing, former world champion Jackie Stewart wasn't alone in suggesting that Jenson was taking his eye off the ball.

When presented with a mechanical package that isn't capable of victory, all a driver can do to preserve his reputation is to be faster than his team-mate. And this Jenson failed to do over the first six races, being outqualified five to one. There had even been talk of making him stand down. This wasn't as sinister as it sounded, but the reaction to a shoulder injury he'd picked up at Sepang. However, it was the sort of setback Jenson didn't need, especially with more hotshots arriving on the scene.

The races in the first half of the year had to be treated as test sessions, with Jenson praying for evolution parts. However, he was also praying for improved form, with technical director Mike Gascoyne reckoning that the performance discrepancy with team-mate Giancarlo Fisichella was down to Jenson not being smoother into corners or so aggressive on the brakes. His only points came from fifth at Hockenheim, right on Fisichella's tail.

One thing that Jenson was wise not to do was to criticise the team, the chassis or the engine. Had he done so, a meeting on the day after the Belgian GP – in which Fisichella had come third, while he'd crashed – could have had a detrimental outcome. The fact that he outqualified Fisichella next time out at Monza may have had more to do with Fisichella having mechanical bothers, but Jenson seemed to be more 'on it', finally being permitted to do a fulsome number of laps in practice. The engine had been given more grunt, too. But Jenson undid all the good work when he took out Jarno Trulli's Jordan at the first chicane.

Rest assured, Jenson will bounce back, with the thought that he can't afford another year like 2001 as Fernando Alonso is waiting in the wings. That, and the desire to prove Irvine wrong...

Jenson's quick step

Jenson was a typical karting hotshot, winning almost every category he entered from the age of 11 onward. With a European title secured in 1997, he moved to cars in 1998 and won the British Formula Ford title. Competitive in Formula Three, he was tipped to stay on in 2000, or perhaps try Formula 3000, but a last-minute deal saw him graduate to Formula One with Williams at the age of 20. Showing remarkable maturity and no little speed, he peaked with fourth in the German GP, but found himself squeezed out to make way for Juan Pablo Montoya.

JAGUAR RACING

NO CREAM FOR THIS CAT

Jaguar Racing is desperate to promote a better image, and it will do this only if major progress has been made over the winter. The finance is in place, but has the team got the right ingredients to advance?

In Control: Niki Lauda assumed sole command midway through the 2001 season when Bobby Rahal was fired

Last year's mantra was that Jaguar Racing would never again take a conservative approach to design. The problem with the Jaguar R2 was that it was a conservative design, perhaps as a result of outgoing Jaguar chairman Neil Ressler saying that he wanted a "reliable" car after the team's endless retirements in 2000. It was also too heavy and too slow, but it was helped on occasion by its Michelin rubber, especially as races progressed and the French tyres became more competitive. Yet, while they were not the fastest cars, they were no more reliable either. In fact their reliability was worse...

Knowing that a third year of the same won't wash well with parent-company Ford, Jaguar spent last year trying to recruit a 'name' designer – someone to lead the design team with support from aerodynamicist Mark Handford and John Russell. Yet this also proved to be a nightmare. Aiming high, Jaguar tried to wrest Adrian Newey from McLaren. But, at the eleventh hour, he was persuaded to stay on, having to renege on a deal with his long-standing friend Bobby Rahal in order to do so. Soon after this, Rahal lost his job as team boss. Niki Lauda assumed complete control after a curious doubled-up relationship with Rahal was brought to an end by the firing of the American former racer last autumn.

While Rahal had been brought in by Ressler, Lauda was appointed by the incoming Wolfgang Reitzle, put in a position of running the group comprising Jaguar Racing, Cosworth and Pi, with Rahal focusing solely on the team. Lauda saw his first main job was to establish a wind tunnel. There was also the matter of locating a suitable base once their plans to build at Silverstone were halted by environmentalists. The latter quest continues, but after having to make do with the hassle of using Swift's wind tunnel in California, Jaguar will have its own wind tunnel in England.

The twin-headed management is gone, with Rahal being fired on the premise that he was too busy with his businesses and racing team in the USA to spend enough time at the helm, and that he'd attempted to offload Eddie Irvine to Jordan after it had fired Heinz-Harald Frentzen. Rahal said that he'd only done it as a joke to old friend Eddie Jordan. The most likely reason seems to be

that Rahal had been put in charge for the sole purpose of luring Newey from McLaren.

Niki Lauda immediately assumed sole charge of the Jaguar team, and Lauda then spent the rest of the year seeking someone to be his right-hand man. That person was Ford Rally engineer Gunther Steiner, who came across in December after the rally season ended.

Then, late last autumn, Jaguar's bid to land the services of the Williams duo of Gavin Fisher and Geoff Willis ended in further disappointment, with Fisher electing to stay and Willis heading instead to BAR. Amid all this restructuring, the fact that Irvine and Pedro de la Rosa are staying on as drivers has passed by almost unnoticed.

FOR THE RECORD

Country of origin	England
Team base	Milton Keynes, England
Website	www.jaguar-racing.com
Active in Formula One	From 1997 (as Stewart)
Grands Prix contested	83
Wins	1
Pole positions	1
Fastest laps	0

DRIVERS + RESULTS 2001

Driver	Nationality	Races	Wins	Pts	Pos
Eddie Irvine	Northern Irish	17	-	6	12th
Pedro de la Rosa	Spanish	13	-	3	16th
Luciano Burti	Brazilian	4	-	-	-

CAR SPECIFICATIONS

Team principal	Niki Lauda
Technical director	Steve Nichols
Team manager	Gunther Steiner
Chief designers	Mark Handford & John Russell
Chief engineer	Mark Ellis
Test drivers	James Courtney & Andre Lotterer
Chassis	Jaguar R3
Engine	Cosworth V10
Tyres	Michelin

Scarcely in the points

Jaguar got both their cars to the finish of last year's opening round but struggled over the next few races. It wasn't just reliability that they had to worry about, or the fact that they'd struggle for grip until rubber had been laid down on the track, but the fact that there were all sorts of Machiavellian goings-on, with de la Rosa being signed as test driver with the promise of a race seat for 2002, thus unsettling number-two driver Luciano Burti. In fact, Burti left after four races and moved to Prost with an eye on a more secure future, with de la Rosa filling his seat.

Engineer Mark Ellis earned rave reviews from Irvine, who said that Mark had spent the early part of the year firefighting to sort the team that he'd taken over. Irvine said that the changes were needed and that his opinions may be unpopular, but that he would guarantee that he would be around in 2002 while others wouldn't.

After a disappointing start to the year that produced a best result

of seventh for Irvine in Austria, changes to the R2 were brought forward by a race, arriving at Monaco. And how this transformed the team, with its new diffuser and associated aerodynamic package adding downforce aplenty. Irvine duly did the rest by qualifying in sixth place and finishing third.

After a dire weekend at the Belgian GP in which Irvine was involved in a huge accident with Burti, de la Rosa brought cheer with fifth at Monza. Next up, Irvine was promoted to fourth at Indianapolis when Trulli was disqualified, moving Jaguar up to equal seventh with Benetton in the constructors' championship. But this became fifth when Trulli was reinstated a month later, dropping Jaguar to eighth.

The quest for glory

Jaguar Racing is in the record books as having existed only since 2000, but it was running for three years before that as the Stewart team. And, for all the money that's been thrown at the team by Ford, it has never matched Stewart's results that included second for Rubens Barrichello in the 1997 Monaco GP, then peaked with first and third for Johnny Herbert and Barrichello at the Nürburgring in 1999 – helping the team to fourth place in the constructors' championship ahead of Williams. Herbert was joined by Irvine when the team became Jaguar in 2000, and their best result until last season was when Irvine was fourth, again at Monaco.

Remember Me?: Eddie Irvine joined his former Ferrari team-mate Michael Schumacher on the podium at Monaco. However, the flamboyant Jaguar driver was to score only once more all season

EDDIE IRVINE

THIRD TIME LUCKY

Irvine is running out of time to turn Jaguar into a competitive team. This is his third year with the team and, although he is great friends with team boss Niki Lauda, keeping his motivation is going to be hard unless results start to flow in 2002.

When people talk of Eddie, they talk of girl-chasing or of the amount that he's being paid to lead Jaguar's thus-far futile attack. However, Eddie appeared to be in love last year – curtailing his activity in the first matter – and then he pointed out that he'd turned his back on a £6.6 million pay-out when he elected to stay for a third year rather than return to Jordan (as had been suggested by Bobby Rahal before the American parted company with the team soon after he'd offered the Ulsterman's services). This was two years' severance pay...

Propelling Jaguar out of the midfield is no overnight job, as shown by the fact that the driver who scored 74 points for Ferrari in 1999 has scored just 10 since. However, Eddie will be hoping that the designers are less conservative this time, as last year was a struggle. Examine Eddie's results from the early races, and an eleventh place followed by four retirements wasn't good. As late as the sixth round, however, Eddie was frustrated by a lack of development. "The car is the same car that hit the track at the beginning of the year. Cosworth have made good steps forward with the engine, but the team haven't made good steps with the car," he said.

Third place at Monaco gave the team a huge fillip, but it seemed to show how hard Eddie was trying rather than indicating any progress that the team had made with the car. This was shown by the fact that he scored just once more in the remaining ten races, with fifth at the United States GP a highlight in a string of retirements.

The low point came at the Belgian GP when he collided with Luciano Burti at the almost flat-out Blanchimont kink. Although Eddie spun harmlessly, the Brazilian's Prost was buried under the tyre wall and many thought he'd been killed. It was a startling accident which he was extremely fortunate to survive, and it was one that shook even the outwardly tough Irvine.

His own boss

Eddie didn't come from a wealthy background and traded in second-hand cars to finance his Formula Ford. Landing a works Van Diemen drive was the making of him, and Eddie jumped from there to Formula Three, shining enough in 1988 to move straight to Formula 3000. Run by Eddie Jordan, he ranked third in 1990, but no Formula One drives were offered so he headed to Japan to race Formula 3000 there. Late in 1993, he was given his Formula One break by Jordan, not only scoring on his debut but getting punched by Ayrton Senna...

His move to Ferrari in 1996 was a surprise, but Eddie was very much the number two in a fractured team. However, as Ferrari advanced, so did Eddie. He scored his first win in Australia in 1999, then became team leader when Michael Schumacher broke a leg. He was only beaten to the title when Mika Hakkinen won the final round.

Spray Boy: Eddie Irvine is considerably more serious about his racing than some people think

PEDRO DE LA ROSA

TRACK NOTES

Nationality	**SPANISH**
Born	**FEBRUARY 24, 1971,**
	BARCELONA, SPAIN
Website	**www.pedrodelarosa.com**
Teams	**ARROWS 1999–2000**
	JAGUAR 2001–2002

On the sidelines at the start of last season, Pedro de la Rosa not only landed a drive with Jaguar but then did his career no harm at all by outpacing his team-leader Eddie Irvine. No wonder de la Rosa's been kept on for 2002.

Pedro de la Rosa doesn't have a high profile outside his native Spain. Indeed, he's a quiet and thoughtful individual, but an intelligent one too, who also happens to be a very good driver. This was shown by the fact that he outqualified his better-known team-mate Eddie Irvine six times in the 13 races they contested together.

To make progress this year, Pedro is going to have to harness all his renowned development skills to hone the new R3 into a car more competitive than last year's R2, and also to hope that the team starts to function on a higher plane in every department.

A mix-up over the winter of 2000/2001 – in which he was expected to stay on at Arrows but was trumped when Enrique Bernoldi brought a raft of Red Bull cash – left Pedro without a drive for last season. He was about to make do with a test deal with Prost but, at the eleventh hour, became Jaguar's test driver. He wasn't kept on the sidelines for long, however, taking a race seat when their number-two driver Luciano Burti moved across to Prost after the French team had dropped Gaston Mazzacane.

The Spaniard took a while to learn the car following minimal testing, but he was in the points on his fourth outing, in the Canadian GP. Bolstered by this performance, Pedro started to outqualify his team-mate, but the results remained disappointing until the Italian GP yielded a rare run to points, for fifth place. Pedro was clear as to why this happened, saying: "It was because we finally put together a good performance for a whole meeting. Before, we would either be good in qualifying but not in the race or *vice versa*." So, continuity will clearly be a key to progress in 2002.

Showing eastern promise

Like many of his era, Pedro had to head east to make it in the west. His early career was a trail of championship-winning success through Formula Ford in Spain in 1990, then Formula Renault in the 1992 British and European series with backing from a national scholarship. However, he was tripped up by running with an uncompetitive Renault engine in British Formula Three. A move to Japan put Pedro back on track as he landed the Japanese Formula Three title in 1995. Then, two years later, he won the country's premier single-seater title in Formula Nippon. A test driver for Jordan in 1998, he was unable to land a race seat until 1999 when Arrows signed him and, although he showed great flashes for the team in 2000 – running third in the Austrian GP – he lost his ride for 2001. But, after testing for Prost, he was snapped up after the first four grands prix to replace Burti at Jaguar.

Pensive: de la Rosa looks for perfection

CAREER RECORD

First Grand Prix	**1999**
	AUSTRALIAN GP
Grand Prix starts	**46**
Grand Prix wins	**0**
best result: fifth, 2001 Italian GP	
Poles	**0**
Fastest laps	**0**
Points	**6**
Honours	**1997 FORMULA NIPPON**
	CHAMPION, 1995 JAPANESE
	FORMULA THREE CHAMPION,
	1992 EUROPEAN & BRITISH
	FORMULA RENAULT CHAMPION,
	1990 SPANISH FORMULA
	FORD CHAMPION

PROST

HANGING ON IN THERE

Prost had been thought unlikely to make it through last winter, as owner Alain Prost faced up to massive debts.

Full Power Ahead: Prost had to hit the close-season at a run to ensure its survival into 2002 as it sorted the finances needed to continue

So bad were Prost's financial worries in 2001 that talk surfaced of them not being able to complete last season. They hung on, only to go into receivership in November. The suitors closed in but faded away again, leading to a deadline of mid-January as to whether Prost would continue. With a week left before this deadline, a consortium of French businessmen with $40m to invest popped up, but nothing was confirmed as this book closed for press.

At the start of 2001, Alain Prost knew his team was short of cash, otherwise he wouldn't have employed Gaston Mazzacane as number two to Jean Alesi. However, Prost fired him when he qualified 2.3 seconds slower than Alesi at Imola. Replacement driver Luciano Burti even outqualified Alesi in their first two races together. As effective as ever in getting to the finish, usually in the top 10, Alesi became increasingly vocal that Prost would make no progress until it made aerodynamic changes. Monaco produced Prost's first point since 1999 when Alesi came sixth. He went one better in Canada, but only one more point would follow – for his sixth place at Hockenheim – as the team ran out of money to fund testing. At the German GP, rumours abounded that Prost was a week from bankruptcy. Finance was found, but Alesi moved to Jordan, swapping with Heinz-Harald Frentzen. He qualified fourth at Spa, but stalled. This was nothing next to Burti suffering a huge accident. He survived, but doctors kept

him away for the rest of the season. This opened the door for Tomas Enge, who stepped up from Formula 3000 with welcome cash.

When Prost was Ligier

Prost spent much of its life under another name, only changing when former world champion Alain Prost took it over in 1997. Before that, it was named after 1960s Formula One racer Guy Ligier. It started life in 1976, with Jacques Laffite scoring the first of Ligier's nine wins in 1977. Their best year was 1979 when Laffite and Patrick Depailler won three of the first five races, although Laffite went into the 1981 finale with an outside chance of the title. Its final win came in Monaco in 1996 courtesy of Olivier Panis.

FOR THE RECORD

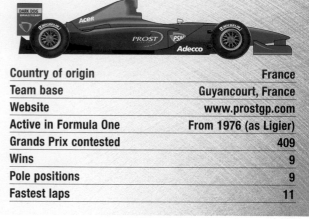

Country of origin	France
Team base	Guyancourt, France
Website	www.prostgp.com
Active in Formula One	From 1976 (as Ligier)
Grands Prix contested	409
Wins	9
Pole positions	9
Fastest laps	11

DRIVERS + RESULTS 2001

Driver	Nationality	Races	Wins	Pts	Pos
Jean Alesi *	French	12	-	5	14th
Luciano Burti	Brazilian	10	-	-	-
Tomas Enge	Czech	3	-	-	-
Heinz-Harald Frentzen*	German	5	-	6	12th
Gaston Mazzacane	Argentinian	4	-	-	-

* Two of Alesi's points were scored when he joined Jordan, while all of Frentzen's points came with Jordan before joining Prost

CAR SPECIFICATIONS

Team principal	Alain Prost
Technical director	Henri Durand
Team manager	Joan Villadelprat
Chief designer	Jean-Paul Gousset
Chief engineer	Vincent Gaillardot
Test driver	tba
Chassis	Prost AP05
Engine	Acer Ferrari V10
Tyres	Michelin

JOS VERSTAPPEN*

A LAST-MINUTE TRANSFER

Jos Verstappen expected to stay on with Arrows, but his career looked set for yet another twist as we closed for press.

CAREER RECORD

First Grand Prix 1994 BRAZILIAN GP	
Grand Prix starts	91
Grand Prix wins	0
best result: third,	
1994 Hungarian GP, Belgian GP	
Poles	0
Fastest laps	0
Points	17
Honours	1993 GERMAN FORMULA
THREE CHAMPION, 1992 BENELUX	
FORMULA OPEL CHAMPION, 1991	
BELGIAN 125cc KART CHAMPION,	
1989 EUROPEAN INTERCONTINENTAL	
KART CHAMPION, 1986 DUTCH	
JUNIOR KART CHAMPION	

Jos had been confirmed as an Arrows driver for 2002, but by the end of 2001, with Arrows in financial peril, Heinz-Harald Frentzen was tipped to take his place, with Jos heading either to Prost or Minardi. His experience remains valued, but most teams want an established winner or an up-and-coming star, preferably with a budget.

Despite driving for midgrid Arrows last year, Jos overtook more cars than anyone, as he'd start with a light fuel load. However, the extra pit-stop always cost him. His most impressive charges were at Sepang and the A1-Ring, climbing as high as second position in both races before dropping back.

A rocket-like ascent

Jos won immediately in Formula Opel after graduating from karts in 1992. He won the German Formula Three title in 1993 and flew

Nationality	DUTCH
Born	MARCH 4, 1972,
	MONTFORT, HOLLAND
Website	www.verstappen.nl
Teams	BENETTON 1994
	SIMTEK 1995
	ARROWS 1996 & 2000–2001
	TYRRELL 1997
	STEWART 1998

in a Formula One test with Arrows, leading to a test drive with Benetton that became a race seat when JJ Lehto was injured. A pair of thirds followed in 1994 – a year marked by his being burned in a frightening pit fire. Jos raced for Simtek in 1995 until that team folded, Arrows in 1996, Tyrrell in 1997 and Stewart in 1998. With no ride in 1999, he got back to Formula One with Arrows in 2000.

PROST NO.2

THE LAST OF THE SIGNINGS

Financial uncertainty meant this signing was made only once the team had guaranteed its survival through into 2002.

The big question as last autumn turned to winter was not so much who would drive for Prost as whether the team would survive into 2002.

As the days ticked by, Prost's number one driver Heinz-Harald Frentzen became worried that the team might fold and leave him without a drive for 2002, so he started talking to Arrows.

Frentzen said all along that he'd only been for a brief visit to Arrows and that he planned to stay with Prost. However, the longer the team stayed in financial peril, the more likely it became that he'd move on.

The team's late-season number two Tomas Enge even started being courted by Formula 3000 teams again as the team faltered in financial peril, but he was always expected to be in the hunt for the second ride, regardless of who took over the team, bringing welcome money from his sponsors from the Czech Republic.

As winter deepened, no one was sure who'd become number one if Frentzen quit.

There was talk of Flavio Briatore placing his new test driver, Fernando Alonso, with Prost so that he could continue to gain race experience in preparation for racing for Renault Sport in 2003 alongside his testing for Renault Sport through the season ahead.

Formula 3000 runner-up Mark Webber was also mentioned, but the team really wanted someone with Formula One experience – failing that, someone with the right budget, and the tall Australian was short in that department.

Among those in the reckoning were India's Narain Karthikeyan, French hotshot Jonathan Cochet – a real favourite of Alain Prost – or any one of three Brazilians, namely Enrique Bernoldi if he didn't stay at Arrows, Formula 3000 ace Antonio Pizzonia or former BAR racer Ricardo Zonta. Yet, such is life at the back of the grid, that a little-known driver with a large wallet could pip them all.

* denotes driver being only a provisional signing at the time of going to press

ARROWS

ANXIOUS TO PLEASE

Arrows is hoping that with Cosworth engines instead of last year's Asiatechs, they will be more competitive in 2002.

Jos Verstappen was confirmed last summer as an Arrows team member for 2002. Yet, such was the team's financial turmoil that his drive remained in doubt, with Heinz-Harald Frentzen tipped to take his place if Prost folded. Indeed, with extra investment from Red Bull, Enrique Bernoldi looked more likely than Jos to stay, although there was talk that it might be the Brazilian who would stand down to admit Frentzen. One definite change, though, is the fact that Arrows is trading up to Cosworth engines.

Arrows suffered from a lack of power from its Asiatechs last year as they were the Peugeots of old by another name, and were another year away from the top engines. However, that didn't stop Jos running second for a while at Sepang. That was in the wet, though, and he only caught people's attention again when he took out race-leader Juan Pablo Montoya after being lapped at Interlagos. His slip from the limelight drew attention away from the fact that rookie Enrique was matching him for pace. Jos made waves in Austria when he made the most of starting with a light fuel load to reach second. Yet, he had to pit twice compared with everyone else's once, and fell to sixth. Enrique kept improving, but if there was mechanical grief to have, he had it. His big day came at Monaco where he kept McLaren's David Coulthard behind him for lap after lap.

Worried by financial problems, Arrows looked to sell its wind tunnel to Jaguar Racing, but this fell through. Walkinshaw denied that Dietrich Mateschitz of Red Bull was set to buy a controlling share with a long-term view to running two American drivers, but a scholarship programme to develop young American talent is underway. It was then announced that Red Bull would also be backing Team Cheever's cars in the Indy Racing League to boost its brand in the USA. Furthermore, Cheever's nephew, Formula Three racer Richard Antinucci, is tipped to test for Arrows.

FOR THE RECORD

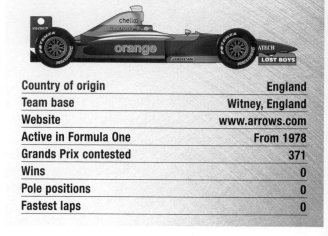

Country of origin	**England**
Team base	**Witney, England**
Website	**www.arrows.com**
Active in Formula One	**From 1978**
Grands Prix contested	**371**
Wins	**0**
Pole positions	**0**
Fastest laps	**0**

DRIVERS + RESULTS 2001

Driver	Nationality	Races	Wins	Pts	Pos
Enrique Bernoldi	**Brazilian**	17	-	-	-
Jos Verstappen	**Dutch**	17	-	1	18th

CAR SPECIFICATIONS

Team principal	**Tom Walkinshaw**
Technical director	**Mike Coughlan**
Team manager	**Mick Ainsley-Cowlishaw**
Chief designer	**Sergio Rinland**
Chief engineer	**Greg Wheeler**
Test driver	**tba**
Chassis	**Arrows A23**
Engine	**Cosworth V10**
Tyres	**Bridgestone**

Still waiting for victory

A breakaway from Shadow formed Arrows in 1978. Going into its twenty-fifth year, Arrows has never won a race. Yet it nearly did so in only its second appearance, at the South African GP, when Riccardo Patrese was thwarted by engine failure when leading. The only other time an Arrows has looked set for victory was when Damon Hill's faltering car was overtaken by Jacques Villeneuve's Williams on the final lap of the 1997 Hungarian GP. In between, the team has run the likes of Thierry Boutsen, Derek Warwick, Michele Alboreto and Mika Salo. But even a change of ownership from Jackie Oliver to Tom Walkinshaw in 1996 has failed to take Arrows that extra step.

Nosing Ahead: Arrows are aiming to move into the heart of the midfield with Cosworth engines that will outstrip their 2001 units

HEINZ-HARALD FRENTZEN*

A FALL FROM GRACE

Heinz-Harald fell from grace in 2001, ending up at Prost. He needs better luck.

CAREER RECORD

First Grand Prix	1994 BRAZILIAN GP
Grand Prix starts	129
Grand Prix wins	3
	1997 San Marino GP
	1999 French GP, Italian GP
Poles	2
Fastest laps	6
Points	160
Honours	1997 FORMULA ONE RUNNER-UP, 1989 GERMAN FORMULA THREE RUNNER-UP, 1988 GERMAN FORMULA OPEL CHAMPION, 1984 GERMAN JUNIOR KART CHAMPION

Heinz-Harald was in demand for 2002, with Prost, Arrows and Minardi all seeking his signature. As we closed for press, this experienced German's future was in the balance. Should Prost have failed to survive, he'll most likely move to Arrows.

After scoring points in three of the first four races last year, he never scored again and Jordan dropped him before the German GP. A swap with Jean Alesi took him to Prost and he qualified fourth at Spa, but stalling on the grid undid all his good work.

A glorious past

Formula Opel champion in 1988, he was equal second with Michael Schumacher in German Formula Three in 1989, then raced in F3000. Racing sportscars for Mercedes was followed by F3000 in Japan before reaching

Formula One with Sauber in 1994. Third in the 1995 Italian GP was followed by winning the 1997 San Marino GP for Williams. He won the 1999 French and Italian GPs for Jordan.

ENRIQUE BERNOLDI

BETTER THAN EXPECTED

Bernoldi surprised insiders last year with his speed. He needs to score in 2002.

CAREER RECORD

First Grand Prix	2001 AUSTRALIAN GP
Grand Prix starts	0
Grand Prix wins	0
	best result: 8th, 2001 German GP
Poles	0
Fastest laps	0
Points	0
Honours	1998 BRITISH FORMULA THREE RUNNER-UP, 1996 EUROPEAN FORMULA RENAULT CHAMPION, 1991 BRAZILIAN KART CHAMPION, 1990 BRAZILIAN KART CHAMPION

A patchy record in the junior formulae – in which he'd shone in Formula Three, but been inconsistent in Formula 3000 – didn't suggest that Enrique would make it to Formula One. But he did, and outqualified Verstappen ten to seven. With backing from Red Bull, his place for a second year was confirmed as we closed for press.

Schooled in Europe

A double Brazilian kart champion, Enrique graduated to car racing in 1995, ranking fourth in Italy's Formula Europa Boxer series. He cleaned up in the 1996 Formula Renault Eurocup, then raced in British Formula Three in 1997, winning once. In 1998, Enrique won

four of the first five races, then won only once again and lost out in the title battle with Mario Haberfeld. He raced for the Red Bull Junior Team in Formula 3000 in 1999 and 2000, but fourth was his best result. He also tested for Sauber before being beaten to their second seat by Räikkönen.

---

* denotes driver being only a provisional signing at the time of going to press

MINARDI

Minardi has come far in a year, not only surviving but landing a works engine deal for 2002.

In the Black: Minardi started last year in the red, but Stoddart turned the team around

FOR THE RECORD

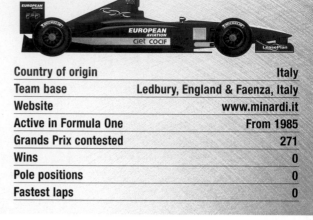

Country of origin	Italy
Team base	Ledbury, England & Faenza, Italy
Website	www.minardi.it
Active in Formula One	From 1985
Grands Prix contested	271
Wins	0
Pole positions	0
Fastest laps	0

DRIVERS + RESULTS 2001

Driver	Nationality	Races	Wins	Pts	Pos
Fernando Alonso	Spanish	17	-	-	-
Tarso Marques	Brazilian	14	-	-	-
Alex Yoong	Malaysian	3	-	-	-

CAR SPECIFICATIONS

Team principal	Paul Stoddart
Sporting director	Rupert Manwaring
Technical director	Gabriele Tredozi
Team manager	Tony Lees
Chief designer	John Davis
Chief engineer	tba
Test driver	tba
Chassis	Minardi PS02
Engine	Asiatech V10
Tyres	Michelin

Last year, Paul Stoddart rescued Minardi in the weeks leading up to the opening race and, if dynamism was everything, he would have propelled the team away from the back of the grid. This year, its big boost from sponsor Magnum, which will be investing £70 million over four years, and its works engine deal means that money has been freed up for testing – a luxury in 2001.

Stoddart pushed for a deal with Cosworth, but Arrows beat him to that. He even waited to see if Prost folded and freed up the second Ferrari engine deal before the deal was done with Asiatech. Stoddart even visited Proton, but claimed that his visit to Malaysia's car manufacturer was a social one so the media shouldn't conclude that Proton would add its name to the engine covers... Whatever the case, the arrival of Asiatechs in place of last year's outdated engines from Ford ought to help them towards the midfield.

Yet, last autumn, Flavio Briatore removed Fernando Alonso from the line-up, making him test for Renault Sport instead. There was talk of Heinz-Harald Frentzen filling the gap as Minardi's number one, as he awaited news on whether Prost would survive. Pressing on, Stoddart considered his options of running Tarso Marques, Mark Webber or even the two drivers from Minardi's Formula 3000 team alongside the inexperienced Alex Yoong. Rumours of an Australian sponsor boosted Webber's chances of breaking into Formula One.

Minardi's 2001 highlights include Alonso marking himself out as one of Formula One's coming-men. His best result was only tenth, but outqualifying more-fancied drivers in more-fancied cars impressed many. Marques appeared to overdrive, though, and he was replaced by Yoong before the Italian GP. The low point was when technical director Gustav Brunner quit for Toyota. His number two, Gabriele Tredozi, stepped up, and he's been joined by John Davis.

Life at the tail

Minardi made the move up from Formula Two in 1985, with Pierluigi Martini and Alessandro Nannini its early standard bearers. It took until 1988 for Minardi to score a point. But Martini caught the eye by leading the 1989 Portuguese GP then qualifying on the front row at Phoenix in 1990 thanks to Pirelli's special qualifying tyres. Using ex-works Ferrari engines in 1991, Martini claimed two fourth places, with Christian Fittipaldi managing another one in 1993. But, apart from Luca Badoer being cruelly deprived of another fourth place at the Nürburgring in 1999, it's been downhill from there.

ALEX YOONG

MALAYSIA'S MAIN MAN

Alex Yoong is a godsend for the Malaysian GP: a home-grown driver to help boost the race-day crowd.

Massive backing for the Minardi team from the Malaysian Magnum Corporation has paved the way for Alex Yoong to have a full crack at Formula One in 2002. Last year, only those with a very good knowledge of the international racing scene knew of Alex before he broke into Formula One for the final three grands prix of the season, taking over the second Minardi seat from Tarso Marques. He finished only once, in sixteenth place, but he appeared to be learning, something he will need to do in the year ahead.

The interest from Malaysia – a country previously with a grand prix circuit, but no Formula One driver – is enormous, as Alex explains. "Racing is quite new to Malaysia, so I'm just trying to educate them, to explain that I'm not going to win races straight away," he said.

CAREER RECORD

First Grand Prix	2001 ITALIAN GP
Grand Prix starts	3
Grand Prix wins	0
best result: 16th, 2001 Japanese GP	
Poles	0
Fastest laps	0
Points	0
Honours	
1995 FORMULA ASIA RUNNER-UP	

TRACK NOTES

Nationality	MALAYSIAN
Born	JULY 20, 1976, KUALA LUMPUR, MALAYSIA
Website	www.alexyoong.com
Teams	MINARDI 2001–2002

From small acorns...

Nothing that has gone before in Alex's career suggested that he would make it to Formula One. He started in Formula Asia, came to race in British Formula Renault then British Formula Three from 1998, never reaching the top step of the podium. Still, he advanced to Formula 3000 and later Formula Nippon, but his last win is still from back in 1995 when he was in Formula Asia...

MINARDI No.2

FOUR-WAY BATTLE

Drivers aplenty were considered to join Alex Yoong in Minardi's 2002 line-up.

Many saw Mark Webber – runner-up to Justin Wilson in Formula 3000 last year – as the driver most likely to sign as Minardi's number two driver. The tall Australian has a useful ally: Flavio Briatore. Yes, the man who pulled Fernando Alonso from Minardi's 2002 line-up to make him test driver for his Renault Sport team. Also managed by Briatore, Mark could thus make a straight swap with the Spaniard, having been test driver for Briatore's Benetton team in 2001, especially if a rumoured Australian sponsor signs up.

Another option is Tarso Marques, who was having a second stab at Formula One last year. Although outpaced by Alonso, he managed a better finishing position (ninth) twice. Despite being dropped for the final three races to make way for Alex Yoong, the Brazilian stayed faithful to the team. He's seen as an outside shot.

Also being considered for the number two seat was David Saelens, a Belgian driver who has had an up-and-down career, with tenth in last year's Formula 3000 standings for Minardi's junior team a big disappointment as he never once made it to the podium. He gained further experience by racing for Mercedes in the German Touring Car series.

Andrea Piccini scored just one point in Formula 3000 last year, but conducted a good deal of Formula One testing for Minardi. In fact, he was in the car more often than Alonso or Marques last year... Occasional Prost number two Tomas Enge was also mentioned in despatches.

Outside shots for the number two seat included two drivers with the experience that Stoddart craved to help develop Yoong: Heinz-Harald Frentzen and Jos Verstappen...

Yes, the lead drivers for Prost and Arrows last season were both in Paul Stoddart's sights. But Frentzen appeared to hold all the cards as he decided on whether to stay faithful in financially-beleaguered Prost or jump across to Arrows in place of Verstappen. But holding out for Prost as the team sought a buyer was a risk that could leave him without a drive if Arrows elected to firm up. And, all along, Minardi would have been anxious to sort its second driver for 2002, but mindful of holding out for a driver of the calibre of Heinz-Harald or Jos, a driver with the experience to help develop the team. Neither Heinz-Harald nor Jos would bring big financial backing like some lesser drivers but their experience is worth more.

TOYOTA

NEW FOR 2002

It's not every year that Formula One fans are treated to a new team. And it's rarer still that this team has funding aplenty.

The Press assembled at Paul Ricard last March for the launch of Toyota's Formula One campaign. Planned as an unveiling followed by the team's first test at the French circuit, this was cut short when Mika Salo crashed. Testing soon resumed, although not necessarily with these early cars setting competitive lap times.

Allan McNish had signed as test driver for 2001, but team chief Ove Andersson intimated that the Scot ought to be Salo's partner in 2002. Yet it wasn't until late October that the announcement was made. Toyota's managing director Tsutomu Tomita said: "Allan is fast and gifted with exceptional development potential."

While McNish got his job, others lost theirs. Andre de Cortanze was technical director at the outset, but he was fired last May, with

FOR THE RECORD

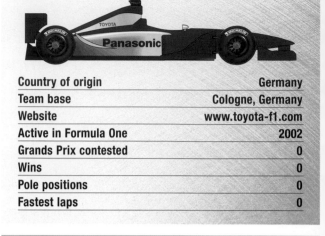

Country of origin	Germany
Team base	Cologne, Germany
Website	www.toyota-f1.com
Active in Formula One	2002
Grands Prix contested	0
Wins	0
Pole positions	0
Fastest laps	0

CAR SPECIFICATIONS

Team principal	Ove Andersson
Team manager	Ange Pasquali
Chief designer	Gustav Brunner
Chief engineer	Humphrey Corbett
Test driver	Ryan Briscoe
Chassis	Toyota TF102
Engine	Toyota V10
Tyres	Michelin

Gustav Brunner being drafted in from Minardi. With a three-year deal for £8 million, it's hard to begrudge the Austrian this opportunity, although it left Minardi team owner Paul Stoddart upset.

There was also much bad feeling in the paddock when it seemed that Toyota was going to ignore the teams' testing ban. However, by mid-September, Toyota had agreed to test only until November 15, the date on which it lodged its entry for this year's championship.

Looking at the ingredients for Toyota's first year, the cars will be fitted with Michelin tyres. Typically frank, Andersson said: "It remains to be seen whether going with Michelin is better than going with Bridgestone, but it was a corporate decision..." This aside, he was also able to say that Toyota had offered him *carte blanche*: "We're starting with a blank sheet of paper," he grinned. "Our target for 2002 is to become respected as a Formula One team. The first year is a working year. We have to face the reality that what we're trying to do is very difficult. What we have to do is to build a platform."

A rallying and enduro background

Toyota is known for its success in the World Rally Championship, with titles for Carlos Sainz in 1990 and 1992 and Juha Kankkunen in 1993 plus manufacturers' titles in 1993, 1994 and 1999. Toyota has also made a major effort at winning the Le Mans 24 Hours, coming close in 1998 and 1999. Toyota has also supplied race-winning engines to the Champ Car series, but this project is being scrapped to help finance its Formula One ambitions.

Scot to Trot: Allan McNish is ready and raring to go after finally being given his long-awaited break in Formula One a decade after his rivals

MIKA SALO

AN EASTERN FAVOURITE

Mika Salo has had a stop-start Formula One career. This time he'll make it stick.

CAREER RECORD

First Grand Prix	1994 JAPANESE GP
Grand Prix starts	94
Grand Prix wins	0
best result: second, 1999 German GP	
Poles	0
Fastest laps	0
Points	31
Honours	1990 BRITISH FORMULA THREE RUNNER-UP, 1988 EUROPEAN FORMULA FORD CHAMPION

A year spent away from racing is a strange career move, but it has worked for Mika Salo, as he concentrated on testing for Toyota and now finds himself as their number one. With 94 grands prix to his name, it's time to prove that he has the speed and the guile to deliver.

After beating Michael Schumacher to the 1988 European Formula Ford crown, he came to Britain to race in Formula Three. His second year in this formula had him chasing Hakkinen hard for the title, ending as runner-up. In Japan, Salo never had a competitive ride in Formula 3000, but got his Formula One break with Lotus at the end of 1994. He shone for Tyrrell in 1995, but the team was on the slide. Flashes of speed shown at Arrows and BAR were confirmed when he

TRACK NOTES

Nationality	FINNISH
Born	NOVEMBER 30, 1966, HELSINKI, FINLAND
Website	www.mikasalo.net
Teams	LOTUS 1994 TYRRELL 1995–1997 ARROWS 1998, BAR 1999 FERRARI 1999, SAUBER 2000 TOYOTA 2002

subbed for Schumacher at Ferrari in 1999 and would have won the German GP, but let team-mate Irvine through. His 2000 season with Sauber wasn't very successful, though.

ALLAN McNISH

HERE AT LAST

It's taken McNish 11 years more than old team-mate Hakkinen to reach this stage.

TRACK NOTES

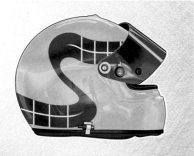

Nationality	SCOTTISH
Born	DECEMBER 29, 1969, DUMFRIES, SCOTLAND
Website	www.allanmcnish.com
Teams	TOYOTA 2002

Everyone in the sport is delighted that Allan has made it to Formula One, as he was one of the quickest who slipped through the net and never got the opportunity that he deserved. Until now, that is...

An intelligent driver, he will not only help develop the Toyota, but ought to be able to get the best out of it in races. Allan himself isn't short of confidence, relishing the task: "I'm driving better than ever. I'm quicker and a lot more experienced in testing and developing cars and racing."

A karting superstar, Allan was tiny when he burst into Formula Ford in 1987, aged 17 but looking 13. He was effective, though, and went on to win the 1988 British Formula Vauxhall title. Pipped to the British Formula Three title in 1989, Allan McNish stepped up to Formula 3000 with aplomb, winning races and landing Formula One test rides with

CAREER RECORD

First Grand Prix	2002 AUSTRALIAN GP
Grand Prix starts	0
Grand Prix wins	0
Poles	0
Fastest laps	0
Points	0
Honours	2000 AMERICAN LE MANS SERIES CHAMPION, 1998 LE MANS 24 HOURS WINNER, 1989 BRITISH FORMULA THREE RUNNER-UP, 1988 BRITISH FORMULA VAUXHALL CHAMPION, 1987 BRITISH JUNIOR FORMULA FORD RUNNER-UP, 1986 BRITISH KART CHAMPION, 1984 SCOTTISH KART CHAMPION, 1983 BRITISH KART CHAMPION, 1982 SCOTTISH KART CHAMPION

McLaren and Benetton. However, the call to race in Formula One never came and Allan's successes in the 1990s were earned in sportscar racing, winning the Le Mans 24 Hours for Porsche in 1998, then the American Le Mans Series title for Audi in 2000.

TOYOTA: F1's NEWEST TEAM

INTO THE FIRING LINE

It's not every year that Formula One gains a new team. It happens even less frequently that a new team is entered by a manufacturer. But, the question is whether serious automotive dollars will be able to guarantee Toyota sporting success in this high-pressure arena.

The Boss: Long-time rally chief Ove Andersson has a lot to consider as Toyota prepares to make a splash in Formula One

If you consider the top teams in Formula One to be well-heeled, then you're right. One glance at their marble-portalled, high-tech headquarters is enough to merit that description. However, when motor manufacturers flex their muscles, these teams are but minnows. Certainly, Fiat has been financing Ferrari for years, but the Italian team is so much part of Formula One's fabric that people tend not to notice Fiat's financial involvement, and all the glory goes to Ferrari. Ford is a newer arrival, back in Formula One with Jaguar Racing since 2000, but the money that the Blue Oval is throwing at Jaguar is a fraction of what Toyota is splashing out on its own new team. Time will tell, but perhaps this relative lack of investment is the reason that Jaguar has been struggling to make an impact. Yet, Toyota is arriving in Formula One with all guns blazing, as it wants to take advantage of the worldwide audience of the sport's highest-profile category. Television airtime sells cars. Winning Grands Prix helps even more, but this might be at least a year or two away, as we shall see later.

First and foremost, Toyota wants to use its involvement with Formula One to help project a more sporting and youthful image. It wants to be thought of as more than a company that sells solid and worthy four-door saloons.

And sport is always the best way to attract younger buyers – a fact acknowledged by Toyota president Fujio Cho, who said: "We're going after the hearts of the younger generation, and Formula One can be seen as part of that strategy." See a red Formula One car and you think Ferrari. From now on, when you see a red and white one, Cho wants you to think only of Toyota. Then, of course, he wants you to buy their cars.

In addition, Toyota wants to steal the thunder from its Japanese rival Honda – a marque that has enjoyed great success in Formula One, especially in the late 1980s when McLaren cleaned up with its engines. And if Toyota succeeds, it will do so doubly, as it's following Ferrari's lead of building both its own chassis and its own engine, rather than following other manufacturers such as Honda, who have been content to focus on supplying their engines to established teams.

So, how is Toyota setting about this steepest of learning curves on the sport's toughest stage? The answer is by planning everything in the utmost detail, and taking years in doing so, then by pumping lots of money into each and every problem that arises in their path. Success in Formula One doesn't come cheaply, so Toyota knows that its programme is going to cost millions upon millions, but the company is serious and will raid its coffers to achieve the desired end result. Although Toyota ranks as the third-largest motor manufacturer in the world behind General Motors and Ford, it's also the most profitable, so the programme won't lack for budget.

Toyota set about lining up key personnel as long ago as 1998, making theirs the longest gestation of any team arriving in Formula One. Unusually, the first name on the sheet was that of a man with no Formula One experience: Ove Andersson. A rally man through and through, he goes back 30 years with Toyota, and this was enough for them to make him team principal. Question Andersson why he has taken on such a huge task at the age of 64, and he answers that the challenge is a "personal target coming true", in a sport with which he thought he'd never be involved.

A driver of repute, Andersson began his long relationship with Toyota by campaigning

a Celica in 1972, when his co-driver was Jean Todt, now sporting director at Ferrari. His greatest result, victory on the 1975 Safari Rally, came in a Peugeot, but when he quit to concentrate on team management he did so with Toyotas, running their cars in the World Rally Championship. This led to the formation of Toyota Team Europe (TTE), a company he sold to Toyota in 1993. Based in Sweden, TTE moved to Brussels in 1975 then to Cologne in 1979. As rallying became more professional and high-tech, an 18,000 sq. ft purpose-built facility was opened in 1987, and this is where the F1 project is based – albeit with an extra 19,000 sq. ft added at a cost of £80 million to accommodate its extra technical requirements.

With eight of the 12 teams – McLaren, Williams, Renault Sport, Jordan, Arrows, BAR, Jaguar and Minardi – based in England, in addition to the majority of the suppliers, insiders consider it strange that Toyota has chosen not to base its Formula One team there, but Andersson has said all along that he's confident they can go it alone in Germany. In the paranoid world of Formula One, some have said that Toyota's decision owes as much to its desire for secrecy as its desire to utilise the facilities and personnel already in place.

Supporting Andersson is Austrian designer Gustav Brunner, who has penned cars for ATS, Alfa Romeo, RAM, Ferrari, Rial, Zakspeed, Leyton House and Minardi since he broke into Formula One back in 1983. His most recent design, last year's Minardi PS01, was a typically tidy and efficient design that was let down by its somewhat underpowered engine. Many insiders are saying that to be a winning team you need cars from a designer of winning cars. In recent world championships that has meant McLaren's Adrian Newey, Ferrari's Rory Byrne or the Williams duo of Gavin Fisher and Geoff Willis. Actually, veteran aerodynamicist Andre de Cortanze had been in charge of the design side before Brunner was enlisted early last year from Minardi.

Pristine Conditions: Toyota Racing's base in Cologne is immaculate, with no expense spared in the manufacturer's quest for glory

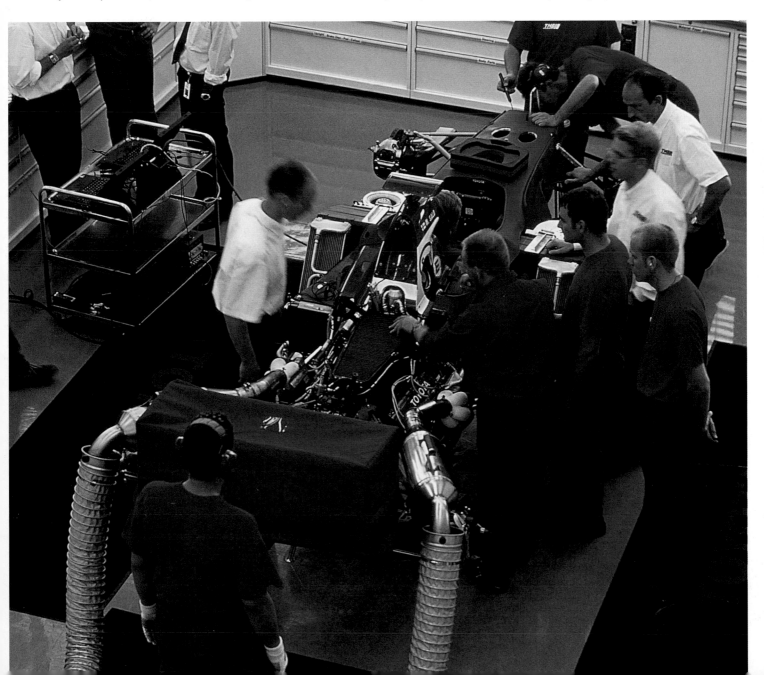

French team manager Ange Pasquali is another man with a rallying background, having co-ordinated Ford's programme before leading Toyota's attack on the Le Mans 24 Hours in the late 1990s. He ran Toyota's Formula One test programme last year and remains at the helm, this time of the race team. All engine development is run by German Norbert Kreyer. Fittingly, there's a Japanese individual in the set-up. Indeed, he is exceedingly important, as Tsutomu Tomita, chairman of Toyota Motorsport, approves all the decisions and signs the cheques... Lower down this hierarchy there are a further 500 employees (50 more than the third-largest team, McLaren), making Toyota the second-largest team after Ferrari.

Just as most people starting a team would seek a winning designer, drivers tend to be chosen in the same way, yet neither of Toyota's drivers has won a Grand Prix. Indeed, although he is talented, one of them hasn't even got a Grand Prix *start* to his name... The chosen pair are led by former Ferrari stand-in Mika Salo, who has been Toyota's choice from the outset. Scottish sportscar expert Allan McNish – a driver who ought to have made it to Formula One a decade ago when he was test driver for McLaren – was named as the team's test driver. Although it was implied that he'd become the number two for 2002, many felt that Heinz-Harald Frentzen or even

Testing, Testing: Mika Salo spent last year pounding around most of the European circuits, gaining valuable mileage in Toyota's development chassis

a Japanese driver would beat him to it. However, Andersson was at pains to explain that this might not be the case: "We've agreed with Toyota that when there's a Japanese driver qualified for a seat, then we'll have them, but not just because they're Japanese," he said. Although Andersson stressed last July that McNish had done enough to make the seat his, it wasn't until October, in the week following the Japanese GP that the Scot was confirmed as Toyota's second driver. In the years ahead, though, both drivers might be discarded for an established Grand Prix winner and an up-and-coming Japanese talent.

With Toyota anxious that no stone should remain unturned in its quest to be competitive, Salo and McNish conducted a huge amount of testing last year. Toyota had actually started testing in 2000, using a Toyota Le Mans car to develop components and to motivate the team. Much of this testing was done at Paul Ricard, former home of the French Grand Prix. From mid-summer 2001 onwards, they visited other European venues. Disappointingly, their lap times were off the pace and didn't appear to be improving, with many a serious push producing a lap that would only just scrape inside the 107% qualifying cut-off at that track. Then, as summer turned to autumn, their deficit came down from more than five seconds off the ultimate pace to two seconds as the development chassis started to catch up with the potential of Toyota's V10 engine – something about which both drivers had always been positive.

The Chosen Pair: Mika Salo and Formula One newcomer Allan McNish will carry Toyota Racing's hopes into the team's maiden season in 2002

Mere mention of testing caused a ruffling of feathers, though, for there was a testing ban in place between the end of October and the end of December. Despite facing charges of unfair play, Toyota stated that it would carry on testing through this period. Its rivals kicked up a fuss, saying that Toyota would be gaining an unfair advantage and that, if it was entering the 2002 World Championship, then it should abide by those regulations. Toyota then compromised and said it would stop testing after November 15, the date on which it had to lodge its championship entry.

The question that everyone was asking last year was how lofty Toyota's ambitions were for this first season. People reckoned that their huge spend would have to be matched by startling results. Yet, everyone involved knows just how hard it is to break into Formula One. Just ask BAR... Through all of this, Toyota remained coy about its likely achievements, with Andersson saying: "We must aim to qualify for all the races. Then, if we can finish a little bit higher up we'll feel that we've done a good job. Our target for 2002 is to become respected as a team."

In addition, unlike BAR – the team that arrived for its first year of Formula One in 1999 with the motto "a tradition of excellence" and then achieved so little – Toyota wants to match or even exceed its aims rather than talk big and fall somewhat flat. So concerned was Toyota about the damage of getting things wrong that even though it ran its engine on a dynamometer for the first time in September

2000, it delayed the project by 12 months, anxious to develop a group of people who could run a racing team as well as those who could build the car and engine. According to Andersson, the timetable by which Toyota must be winning races is 2004, with Toyota hoping to be challenging for the title by 2006.

Toyota's bankrolling of the project has helped the team avoid the soon-to-be-outlawed sponsorship from cigarette companies being found on its bodywork. Title sponsorship has gone instead to the electricals giant Panasonic.

Toyota isn't only sending a cheque to its Cologne motorsport headquarters, however, as it has also struck closer to home by buying the Fuji Speedway. Famed for hosting the 1976 World Championship showdown between James Hunt and Niki Lauda, the track in the foothills of Mount Fuji was visited by Formula One just once more in 1977 before being dropped, with Suzuka later becoming the home of the Japanese Grand Prix. After years of decline, Toyota's injection of cash into Fuji will bring the track up to contemporary Formula One specification, and this will help the track challenge Suzuka for the right to host Japan's Grand Prix later this decade. Indeed, this could be just in time to coincide with Toyota being ready to challenge for race wins or even championship honours. We'll have to wait and see, but remember that money doesn't necessarily buy success in Formula One, as application and expertise are also required to complete the equation.

Get set up for the BRITISH GRAND PRIX

With the ways of setting up a Formula 1 car many and varied, we take a closer look at how teams fine-tune the car's set-up to give their drivers the best handling cars for Silverstone.

Adjusting rear wing:
Differences of pressure above and below wings create downforce

Curved lower surface of wing makes air flow further and faster – air pressure drops

Holes allow wing angle to be adjusted

Silverstone is a medium downforce circuit, a compromise between fast straights and a tricky infield section

End-plates stop air pressure differences migrating around ends of wings, increasing effectiveness

■ High pressure
■ Low pressure

Suspension:
All F1 teams use torsion springs rather than coiled springs. **Twisting motion produces spring effect.** A coiled spring is effectively a coiled torsion bar

Quick change
Torsion bars are quick and easy to change by removing an end cap, sliding out the bar and dropping in a new one. Engineers and drivers choose from a wide range of springs and shock absorber settings. Colour coding at either end of springs denote stiffness. Stiff springs mean better handling but take their toll in tyre wear

The right brakes:
Various thicknesses of carbon fibre discs available up to 28mm. The faster the circuit, the thicker the disc used. **Disc wear can amount to as much as 30% or more during one race**

Disc

Duct

Lo-tech adjustment:
Braking response can be tuned by changing the cooling effect of the brake duct using sticky tape over part of the opening

Fine-tuning engines:
3D engine-management software written to produce specific performance characteristics for Silverstone controlling fuel delivery, timing and air-inlet trumpet length

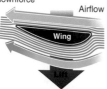

Teams always strive to lower car's centre of gravity. Flattening "V" angle of engine is subject of much research, but engineers get problems with vibration if power strokes are not spaced evenly. **Tight packaging and rigidity are compromised as V gets wider. A 72° V is ideal for V10 engines**

Even timing, crank balanced, 10 x 72¡ = complete cycle

End-view of crankshaft

Gearbox: Each gear ratio individually tailored to suit specific circuit demands. **Engine and gearbox both changed between qualifying and race, and completely rebuilt after it**

Gearboxes fully automatic

The right rubber:
1: Dry tyre 2: Wet tyre. Two dry tyre compounds available at each GP – soft (grip), hard (durability) – and three types of wet tyre, inflated to a relatively soft 20 psi. **Heating tyres is vital to maintain correct pressure at racing speed and temperature.** Too much or too little air pressure increases wear and results in a dramatic loss of pace

Front wing designs:
Balance between front and rear is critical. Many teams have suffered from lack of front end grip this season and expoited a loophole allowing a lower centre to the wing for greater downforce

Setting ride-height:
Rear: 50-60mm. Front: 20-30mm. Under braking, leading edge of undertray may brush tarmac at end of high-speed straight. **Lower ride heights produce more under-car downforce but more than 1mm of wear in "plank" bolted to car floor means disqualification**

10mm plastic "plank"

Three key areas of F1 set-up:
Aerodynamics: **40%**
Engine/gearbox: **40%**

Suspension: 20%
With a good aerodynamic package, the improvements that race engineers are able to find in car set-up can make the difference between winning and losing

A lap of Silverstone

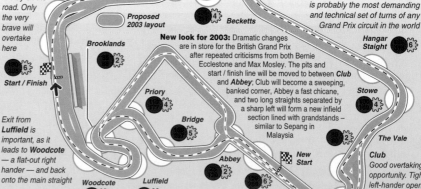

Copse ⚙5

Blind entry, 160mph. Good downforce is vital to stay on the road. Only the very brave will overtake here

Start / Finish

Exit from **Luffield** is important, as it leads to **Woodcote** — a flat-out right hander — and back onto the main straight

Maggotts ⚙6

Brooklands ⚙2

Priory ⚙4

Bridge ⚙5

Abbey ⚙2

Woodcote ⚙5

Luffield ⚙3

Chapel ⚙5

Becketts ⚙4

Proposed 2003 layout

New look for 2003: Dramatic changes are in store for the British Grand Prix after repeated criticisms from both Bernie Ecclestone and Max Mosley. The pits and start / finish line will be moved to between **Club** and **Abbey**; Club will become a sweeping, banked corner, Abbey a fast chicane, and two long straights separated by a sharp left will form a new infield section lined with grandstands – similar to Sepang in Malaysia

New Start

With the exception of **Eau Rouge** at the Belgian Grand Prix, the **Maggotts-Becketts-Chapel** complex is probably the most demanding and technical set of turns of any Grand Prix circuit in the world

Hangar Straight ⚙6

Stowe ⚙4

⚙2

The Vale

Club
Good overtaking opportunity. Tight left-hander opens up on exit, allowing drivers to reach sixth briefly before braking for **Abbey** chicane

⚙6

⚙4

Speed (mph) [100] Gear ⚙4 Racing line ---

© GRAPHIC NEWS   Sources: Williams, Arrows, Jaguar, Silverstone, Autosport

QUICK CHANGE ARTISTS

With races increasingly won and lost in the pit lane, as many as 21 men make up the pit stop crew. Team truck drivers or mechanics at other times, for a few seconds each race these guys, rather than the drivers, get to be the stars.

–1 lap:
Crew takes up positions as driver passes pit and gets signal to come in at end of next lap

–16.3 seconds:
Tyres taken to pit lane wrapped in electric blankets. Choice of compound – harder or softer – made before race. Compound may not be changed during race

–10 seconds:
Driver enters pit lane and activates limiter to keep within speed limit

STOP!
PITS

0.0 | 1.0 | 2.0 | 3.0

0.2 seconds:
Air-hammers in place on wheel nuts

1.0 second:
Front and rear jacks in position, car raised

1.5 seconds:
Fuel hose connected. Red light inside refueller's helmet indicates fuel flowing

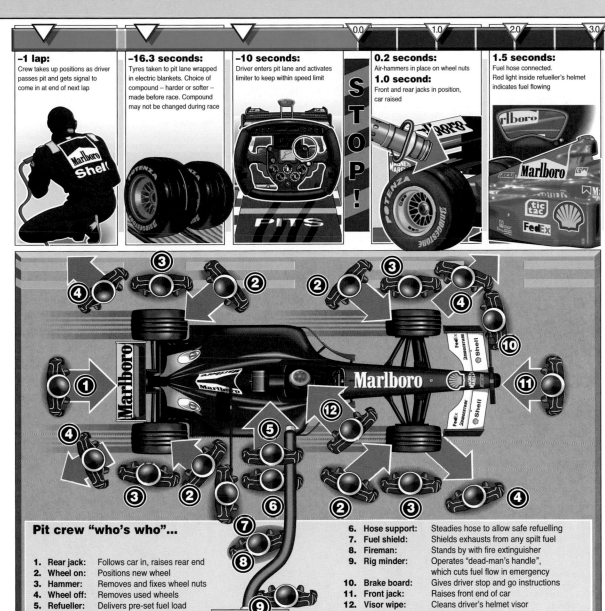

Pit crew "who's who"...

1.	**Rear jack:**	Follows car in, raises rear end
2.	**Wheel on:**	Positions new wheel
3.	**Hammer:**	Removes and fixes wheel nuts
4.	**Wheel off:**	Removes used wheels
5.	**Refueller:**	Delivers pre-set fuel load
6.	**Hose support:**	Steadies hose to allow safe refuelling
7.	**Fuel shield:**	Shields exhausts from any spilt fuel
8.	**Fireman:**	Stands by with fire extinguisher
9.	**Rig minder:**	Operates "dead-man's handle", which cuts fuel flow in emergency
10.	**Brake board:**	Gives driver stop and go instructions
11.	**Front jack:**	Raises front end of car
12.	**Visor wipe:**	Cleans driver's helmet visor

4.0 | 5.0 | 6.0 | 7.0 | 8.0 | 9.0 | 10

2.0 seconds:
"Brakes on" lollipop displayed to driver

2.5 seconds:
Wheels off

3.5 seconds:
New wheels on

3.7 seconds:
Hammers removed. Each wheel-man raises right hand to signal "all-clear"

3.8 seconds:
Jacks lowered

5.5 seconds:
"First gear" board shown, driver prepares to exit pit

1ST

6.5 seconds:
Full fuel load delivered at 12 litres/sec (60 litres), hose disengaged

10.0 seconds:
Car returns to track. Crew returns to garage to reset and replace equipment for next car

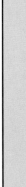

FINANCING THE FORMULA

Besides paying their superstar drivers, up to 250 staff per team and travelling to each event, Formula One outfits have one extra expense that other sports don't. The car – the most expensive, complex and hi-tech item of sporting equipment in the world.

Rear wing: Six sets to start plus development sets throughout season: **£8,000 per assembly**

Bodywork: Repainted after each race: **£4,000**

Monocoque: Body of car. Made from ultra-strong carbon fibre and aluminium honeycomb composite. Minimum eight per season: **£70,000 each**

Exhaust system: **£4,000-£6,000**

Radiators: **£39,000:** Changed after two races

Seat: Six per season: **£2,000 each**

Mirrors: **£300-£400**

Suspension: **£8,000** front/rear

Tyres: **£400** each

Engines: Teams in partnership with manufacturer get engines for free. Ferrari and Arrows build their own. Other teams lease engines – e.g. Renault-Supertec deal, including development, costs £13 million per season

Wheels and hubs: Set of four: **£7,000**

Front wing: Six sets: **£10,000 each**

Brakes, pads and calipers: Decelerating from 200mph to 50mph within 100 metres requires prodigious stopping power. Brakes and pads are made of carbon, calipers from solid aluminium
Disks: **£600**
Pads: **£400**
Calipers: **£10,000**

Shock absorbers: Five sets per car plus development during season: **Set: £4,000**

Gearbox/cogs: Operated either by hydraulics or air, gearboxes are semi-automatic. Gearchanges take 20 milliseconds. Gearbox casting also functions as stress-bearing part of car, supporting rear axle and suspension. 15-17 per season.
Gearbox (inc maintenance): **£150,000**
Set of gear ratios: **£70,000**

Steering wheel: Apart from 'stop' and 'go' pedals, wheel controls all functions. Mechanical parts last whole season, electronics just two races
Wheel: Up to **£10,000**
Steering system: **£3,000**

And the rest...	
Wind tunnel costs	**£14 million**
Telemetry systems	**£80,000+**
Air freight/Travel	**£3.3 million**
Team clothing	**£100,000**
Refuelling rig (inc maintenance)	**£44,000**

Source: F1 News, Science of Speed, Technology of the F1 Car, F1 Mech Tech   © GRAPHIC NEWS

A far cry from the AVERAGE STEERING WHEEL

Once upon a time, a racing car's steering wheel was just that, with the gears close at hand and three pedals on the floor. In today's Formula 1 car, all the controls except throttle and brake pedals are located on the wheel. So let's take an in-depth tour of Michael Schumacher's tool of the trade.

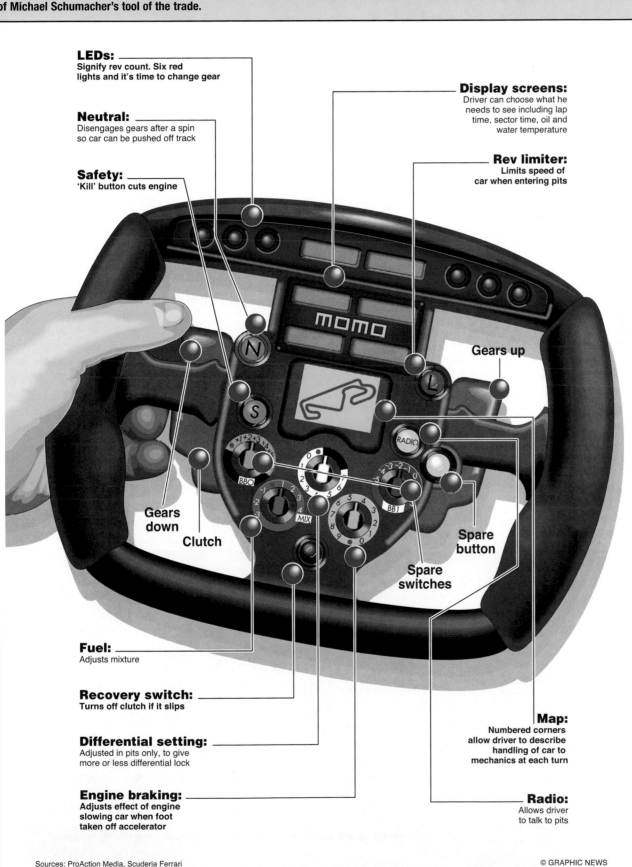

LEDs:
Signify rev count. Six red lights and it's time to change gear

Neutral:
Disengages gears after a spin so car can be pushed off track

Safety:
'Kill' button cuts engine

Display screens:
Driver can choose what he needs to see including lap time, sector time, oil and water temperature

Rev limiter:
Limits speed of car when entering pits

Gears up

Gears down

Clutch

Spare button

Spare switches

Fuel:
Adjusts mixture

Recovery switch:
Turns off clutch if it slips

Differential setting:
Adjusted in pits only, to give more or less differential lock

Engine braking:
Adjusts effect of engine slowing car when foot taken off accelerator

Map:
Numbered corners allow driver to describe handling of car to mechanics at each turn

Radio:
Allows driver to talk to pits

Sources: ProAction Media, Scuderia Ferrari

© GRAPHIC NEWS

SETTING-UP A CAR FOR DIFFERENT GP CIRCUITS

TUNING AND TWEAKING

The world's most advanced racing cars achieve what they achieve only through massive input from the teams' engineers. This is how they go about their work during the course of a Grand Prix meeting, whether at Monaco or Monza.

A team can spend a fortune designing, testing and developing its car and engine for the forthcoming season. Yet, if that team fails to find a suitable chassis set-up, then their efforts will be for nothing. With each of the circuits visited being different in format, and serving up a variety of weather conditions, there's a battle to find the ultimate set-up 17 times during the year.

Indeed, you don't need to have an engineering degree to know that the set-up for a high-speed circuit such as Monza will be very different from one needed for a low-speed, stop-and-go circuit such as Monaco. The set-ups for these circuits will be almost completely opposite in terms of the wing settings and the amount of compliance required in the suspension. However, the method by which the engineers reach what they consider to be the optimum set-up will be remarkably similar, as all teams work to a programme aimed at creating the ultimate set-up over the three days of a Grand Prix meeting.

Since nothing is left to chance in Formula One, where every fraction of a second counts, teams will have a general idea about how to set up their cars before they even leave their bases. After all, they will almost certainly have raced at each circuit the previous year, and will probably have tested there since, too. Rule changes mean that engineers often can't duplicate their set-up from before, but their previous experience will have given them a more-than-general idea. It won't simply be a case of guessing some suspension settings, wing angles and tyre pressures and sending the drivers out to 'see what they can do'.

Furthermore, a team of engineers will have worked on computer modelling back at base – with each circuit's defining co-ordinates plotted in – analysing the theoretical impact of set-up changes. In the case of visiting the Indianapolis Motor Speedway for the first time in 2000, this was all they had to go on. The test team, though, will also have put in mileage at a circuit possessing corners with similar characteristics to the one about to be visited.

Whether visiting the twisty Hungaroring or the frequently flat-out Spa-Francorchamps, there are six main variables on which the

Constant Change: Altering a car's aerodynamics, ride height, suspension, tyres, brakes and gearing can all affect the way it handles

engineers can work: aerodynamics, ride height, suspension, tyres, brakes and gearing. Then, of course, there's that universal variable known as the weather, with a car's handling affected not only by if it's wet or dry, but also by changes in temperature and wind direction as well. Watching the difference in straightline speed down the long start/finish straight on a gusty day at Indianapolis last autumn was a real eye-opener, with a 5mph (8kph) variance, depending on the strength of the gusts. However, one thing that's clear is that no team can afford to lose any time once they arrive at the circuit, as they have a fixed programme to work through, and any delay puts them on the back foot for the rest of the meeting.

The regular programme consists of cars being sent out for a pair of one-hour sessions separated by an hour's break on the Friday, with teams working toward a balanced set-up from which they can develop the often contrasting set-ups that they reckon will work best in qualifying and during the race itself. These set-ups can be markedly different. For example, on a circuit at which the engineers are torn between fitting as little wing angle as possible for good straightline speed and cranking on more wing to help it through the corners, such as Monza, then they will opt for the 'little wing angle' option in qualifying and hope that their drivers can hang on through the corners on their handful of perhaps four flying laps. To run such a set-up in the race would lead to increased tyre wear, as the car would want to slide about through the corners due to the lack of downforce needed to offer it grip. So, for the race itself at such a circuit the engineers would send their drivers out with more wing, in the interest of tyre preservation.

Starting with a car's aerodynamics, pre-event computer simulation will have reduced this from 20 potential settings to around three or four. The cars will start off with a median set-up, with experimentation divided between the team's two cars. This emphasises the importance of having drivers who can identify how a car is handling and even suggest how the settings can be improved. The wing settings will be adjusted either way according to the drivers' findings. For example, if a car is understeering, the engineers will increase the front wing angle to add downforce to the front end in order to boost turn-in.

Closely linked with a car's aerodynamics are its ride height and suspension requirements. In a perfect world, engineers would run their cars as close to the track as the rules allow for maximum aerodynamic efficiency. However, circuits such as Interlagos can be quite bumpy in places so that running the cars low could lead to them grounding their undersides and the drivers losing control momentarily, so they have to be set up high.

It's the suspension settings that make the greatest difference to handling, with engineers able to alter the stiffness of the springs, the dampers and the anti-roll bars to change the handling from anything between oversteer and understeer, according to driver preference. Bear in mind, too, that every driver has a preferred driving style, as some need their cars to turn in as if on rails, while others are happy for them to be 'loose' if that is what's required for a fast lap. Thus, it really helps a team if both of its drivers prefer understeer, for example, so that they can concentrate on developing their cars with that handling characteristic.

All suspension settings will have been tested on a six-post testing rig at the team's base, leaving the team to work through five or six

Watchful Eye: During the Grand Prix weekend drivers waste no chance to observe how their rivals are lapping, what lines they are taking through the corners and whether they can glean any tips on set-up to improve the handling of their own car

set-ups over the Friday and Saturday at a Grand Prix meeting. Tyre wear is affected by changes to springs, dampers and roll-bars, so engineers soften the rear suspension if they have made the car too tyre-hungry. Alternatively, they make it harder if it's not getting enough heat into the tyres for optimum handling. Adding another factor into the equation as engineers choose between tyre compounds, surface abrasiveness varies from circuit to circuit. On top of this, they can alter the handling by raising or lowering the tyre pressures.

Keeping it legal: All cars are measured constantly to check that their dimensions remain within the legal parameters

Teams choose between three or four brake materials according to the characteristics of the circuit, with venues such as Monza demanding heavy braking and therefore requiring thicker discs and pads. As flying laps in qualifying don't require brakes to last a long time, teams can afford to run with thinner discs and pads – unlike in the race, when cars are also heavier with their full fuel load.

The engineers' final consideration is the gearing to use as they look for the gear ratios that will optimise the engine's power curve, while not costing them top speed. A circuit such as Monaco doesn't have a long-enough straight to make top speed a factor, so gearing at Monaco will be aimed at achieving maximum acceleration. Just to make the quest for the ultimate set-up all the more difficult, aerodynamic settings also affect how a car needs to be geared, with Monza's 'flat' wing settings enabling the fitment of a taller top gear.

So, with two hours of practice behind them by Friday lunchtime, the engineers liaise with the drivers and work out further changes to be made for the two 45-minute sessions on the Saturday morning before the vital hour of qualifying kicks off two hours later. A final debrief leads to a decision on a set-up that will be ideal for getting heat into the tyres as fast as possible for a single flying lap. Drivers will aim to fit in four flying laps, each of them in the middle of an 'out lap', 'flying lap' and 'in lap' sequence. Sometimes they try three runs of two flying laps.

With qualifying out of the way, teams turn their attention to the race itself. On Sunday morning, in the half-hour warm-up, teams focus on running their cars with full tanks, hopefully with a set-up that doesn't eat their tyres. This is their final chance to test for the race, save for the handful of laps that drivers can cover after the pitlane opens half an hour before the start, when drivers can drive around to the grid or do several laps by trickling through the pitlane before completing another lap. If it looks as though rain might be in the offing, engineers might crank up the wing or soften the suspension. Other than that, they have to accept that their work is all but done, and that everything is now in their drivers' hands.

Aerodynamic balance
When a car has equilibrium front and rear from the airflow over it. Without this, it will be out of balance and handle either with understeer if there is less downforce over the front, or oversteer if there is less downforce over the rear.

Aerodynamic efficiency
A ratio comparing a car's drag and its downforce.

Bargeboard
The piece of bodywork mounted vertically between the front wheels and the sidepods to smooth airflow around the sides of the car.

Blistering
Occurs with tyres when they overheat and small bubbles in the tread expand and make the surface rubber separate.

Brake balance
The split in the car's braking between front and rear according to a driver's requirements; controlled by a switch in the cockpit.

Centre of pressure
The point at which all of a car's aerodynamic forces are focused.

CFD
Computational Fluid Dynamics; a design function that helps designers to assess airflow over and around a car by simulating fluid flow.

Clean air
Air that isn't turbulent, and which thus offers optimum aerodynamic conditions, as experienced by a car at the head of the field.

Diffuser
The bodywork found at the rear of the underside of a car that is shaped to control the airflow in the most efficient way by accelerating it.

Downforce
The aerodynamic force that is applied in a downwards direction as a car travels forwards. This is harnessed to improve a car's traction and thus its handling through corners.

Drag
The aerodynamic resistance experienced as a car travels forwards.

Drive-by-wire throttle
An electronic throttle control that has superseded the original mechanical pedal control.

ECU
Electronic Control Unit: an engine's electronic brain that adjusts the rate of ignition and fuel flow for optimum engine efficiency.

Endplate
The plate at the end of a wing used to tidy up airflow.

Engine mapping
A technique used in the ECU to counter-adjust the ignition rate and engine timing as either one changes.

Flat spot
When a tyre is worn at a particular spot after a moment of extreme braking or during the course of a spin. A flat spot ruins the car's handling, often causing severe vibration.

Fuel cell
The deformable bag used as a fuel tank.

G-force
A physical force equivalent to one unit of gravity that is multiplied during rapid changes of direction or under acceleration and braking.

Grip
The amount of traction a car has at any given point, thus affecting the ease with which the driver can keep control through corners.

Gurney flap
An adjustable flap on the rear of a wing used to alter the amount of downforce provided by that wing without changing its setting.

Intermediate tyre
A tyre with a more treaded pattern than a dry weather tyre, but less than the wet weather tyre; used in mixed conditions.

Left-foot braking
A style of braking lifted from other motorsports such as rallying, and made popular in Formula One in the 1990s following the arrival of hand clutches, enabling drivers to keep their right foot on the throttle and dedicate their left foot to braking.

Lift
The opposite of downforce, when airflow under the nose, sidepods or wings tries to lift the car from the track.

Monocoque
The single-piece tub in which the cockpit is located, with the engine fixed behind it and the front suspension on either side at the front.

Oversteer
When a car's back end tries to overtake the front end as the driver turns in towards the apex of a corner. This often requires opposite-lock to correct.

Pitch
The fore and aft motion experienced under acceleration, braking and cornering.

Plank
A wooden strip fitted front-to-back down the middle of the underside of all cars to check that they're not being run too close to the track – something that is indicated if the wood is worn away.

Pull rod
A suspension arm from the wheel to the bottom of the shock absorber in which the movement of the wheel over a bump is followed by the arm pulling on the shock absorber.

Push rod
A suspension arm from the wheel to the top of the shock absorber in which the movement of the wheel over a bump is followed by the arm pushing down on the shock absorber.

Reference plane
An imaginary parameter from which all car parts are measured and must be contained, such as the minimum height of the car's floor or the maximum dimensions of the rear wing.

Ride height
The height between the track's surface and the floor of the car, measured at the axle lines.

Roll bar
A torsional spring part fitted to prevent side-to-side roll.

Rollhoop
The metal or carbon-fibre hoop at the rear of the cockpit that protects the driver's head in the event of the car being inverted.

Semi-automatic gearbox
A type of gearbox that requires the driver only to pull on one lever mounted behind the steering wheel to change up a gear and pull another to change down, without having to use a gearlever or clutch pedal.

Sidepod
The part of the car housing the radiators that flanks the sides of the monocoque alongside the driver, and which runs back to the rear wing.

Splash and dash
A flying pit stop in which only minimal fuel is taken on in the closing laps

Telemetry
A system that beams data relating to engine and chassis performance to computers in the pit garage so that the engineers can monitor a car's behaviour.

Traction control
A computerised system that detects if either of a car's driven (rear) wheels is losing traction – in other words spinning – and which transfers more drive to the wheel with more traction, thus using the available power more efficiently.

Turbocharger
A device bolted to the engine that recirculates its own exhaust gases to power a compressor which in turn increases the engine's induction, thus providing extra power. These are no longer permitted

Turbulence
The result of disruption in the airflow, like when it hits a rear wing and its horizontal flow is spoiled.

Turning vane
A panel mounted vertically on the front wing to increase aerodynamic efficiency by deflecting airflow from the front tyres.

Tyre compound
The type of rubber mix used in the construction of a tyre, ranging from soft through medium to hard, with each mix offering different performance and wear characteristics.

Understeer
Where the front end of the car doesn't want to turn into a corner and slides wide as the driver tries to turn in towards the apex and the car under-responds to steering input.

Venturi
A narrowing space through which airflow is forced to accelerate.

Wishbone
V-shaped suspension arm that connects the wheels to the car, with two mounting points on either side of the monocoque at the front and two mounting points on either side of the engine at the rear.

Yaw
The side-to-side motion experienced by a chassis under acceleration, braking and cornering.

REVIEW OF 2001

Michael Schumacher earned the undying love of *tifosi* the world over in 2000 when he became the first Ferrari driver to win the World Championship since Jody Scheckter back in 1979. However, the German's form in 2001 was more impressive still, as he raced to 11 pole positions and 9 race wins. Not only did this give him his fourth world title – putting him equal with Alain Prost and behind only five-time champion Juan Manuel Fangio – but it moved him to the head of the all-time lists for most race wins and most points scored, and the title was his with fully 4 of the 17 grands prix still to run. It was a walkover.

There were times when it looked as though Schumacher would be given a run for his money by a McLaren driver, however. For once, this wasn't Mika Hakkinen but David Coulthard, the Scot stepping up to the plate as the Finn faltered. Indeed, with fortune and occasionally form deserting him, Hakkinen had it in his mind from Monaco to stand down at the end of the season, for a year at least. But Coulthard wasn't able to make the most of assuming the role of McLaren's 'driver most likely to', for the introduction of driver aids – including traction control and launch control – scuppered his chances at several races when the cars in grey, and several others too, simply refused to get off the line. There were few more frustrating moments than watching him pound his steering wheel after his car stalled at the start of the parade lap at Monaco, blowing his valuable pole at this circuit on which overtaking is nigh-on an impossibility. Wins came his way at Interlagos and the A1-Ring, but there were to

Bowing Out: McLaren's Mika Hakkinen wasn't the threat he used to be, winning only twice, and has stood down for a year's sabbatical

be no more, and he was to end the season fighting off the challenges of Ferrari's Rubens Barrichello and Ralf Schumacher from Williams for the unwanted position of being championship runner-up. Unwanted, because all drivers say that winning is everything and nothing else will do.

In truth, Coulthard and Hakkinen struggled because the Mercedes engines behind their shoulders were no longer the class of the field. That honour went to BMW for the engines that they supplied to Williams, and this new-found horsepower was greater even than that at the disposal of the Ferrari drivers. Ralf Schumacher used it to good effect to win three times, starting with victory at Imola. However, by the season's end, his team-mate Juan Pablo Montoya was the faster of the pair, claiming a maiden win at Monza. Watch for both challenging the Ferrari drivers for outright honours in 2002.

Another factor in the Ferrari and McLaren

battle against the newly revitalised Williams challenge was the tyres on their wide wheel rims. It was Bridgestone versus Michelin, and the battle was an interesting one as the Michelins tended to go off after half-a-dozen laps in the race before coming good again after a dozen, enabling those behind to have a chance of passing them. But, if this chance was missed, these drivers were faced with a problem when the French rubber found its sweet spot again.

For many teams, though, this was all slightly irrelevant, as they were never going to challenge the top three teams, and they had to become accustomed to driving with the aim of picking up scraps. Best at doing this was Sauber, with its drivers Nick Heidfeld and rookie Kimi Räikkönen guiding the Swiss team to fourth overall, its best-ever position in the Constructors' Championship. This placed the team ahead of the two Honda-engined teams, Jordan and BAR, with

the former unlucky to miss out on many points scores as Lady Luck frowned on Jarno Trulli time and again. In truth, both of these teams floundered, while the once-great Benetton team was abysmal up to and beyond the mid-point of the season, but found ever more power from its radical Renault engine and from its ever-improving aerodynamic package to end the season looking a points-bet for 2002 when it will be rebadged and reliveried as Renault Sport.

Jaguar disappointed in its second season, but at least it outperformed Prost, Arrows and Minardi, three teams that struggled by on faltering budgets, presenting something of a concern to the sport's governing body as to whether they will survive for long as economic hard times home into view.

All in all, though, it was a great year of racing, with the Japanese finale standing out as one of the best races. Typically, Michael Schumacher took the honours.

THE YEAR IN PICTURES

AUSTRALIAN GP

RED AND BLACK

Two things stand out when looking back at the season-opening Australian GP. Firstly, that Ferrari's Michael Schumacher started his campaign with a win for the second year in succession. Secondly, that the meeting was overshadowed by the unfortunate death of a marshal.

MEMORABLE MOMENT

David Coulthard is a man of honour, but it caused an upset in 1998 when team-mate Mika Hakkinen misheard a radio call and pitted. He was waved through by McLaren, but this dropped him to second behind Coulthard. The Scot had agreed before the race that whichever of them led into the first corner would be allowed to win, and so he waved Hakkinen through, delighting the Finn and sending race promoter Ron Walker into a spin.

Flying Start: Kimi Räikkönen belied his lack of experience to score a point on his debut

With Michael Schumacher and Rubens Barrichello sandwiching David Coulthard (who finished second for McLaren), it was easy to say that Ferrari was in the driving seat as the World Championship kicked off. However, that would ignore the promise indicated by Mika Hakkinen's involvement.

Starting from pole, Schumacher blasted into the lead, but Barrichello was slow away from second on the grid and fell behind Hakkinen, Jordan's Heinz-Harald Frentzen and the Williams of Ralf Schumacher, as Jarno Trulli pushed his Jordan past Coulthard for sixth. This soon changed as Barrichello and Coulthard advanced to third and fourth respectively by the third lap.

Ralf Schumacher wasn't able to fight back, though, as he was hit by Jacques Villeneuve's BAR as they both braked for Turn 3 on lap 5. The Williams went straight on into the gravel trap with its rear wing ripped off. The BAR became airborne and rattled along the wall on the left-hand side of the track. Amazingly, Villeneuve hopped out of his wrecked car, which had been shorn of all four wheels. However, one of them had freakishly killed a marshal by slotting through a small gap cut in the fence to allow marshals access to the track in case of an incident.

The Safety Car withdrew on lap 16 and Michael Schumacher opened up a gap between himself and Hakkinen. Ten laps later, the pressure was off as Hakkinen's suspension failed and pitched him into the wall. McLaren boss Ron Dennis later claimed that the Finn had been running with a heavy fuel load and could have won the race. Indeed, Coulthard was using a similar tactic, and it did steal him a march on the Ferrari duo.

The Scot made the most of Minardi debutant Fernando Alonso apparently not seeing the arrival of Barrichello, and nipped by the Brazilian into Turn 3. He then closed in on Schumacher, but the three-time World Champion had things under control and did just enough to win, with Barrichello crossing the line a further 31 seconds behind.

Olivier Panis was fourth across the line, offering BAR a reason for some cheer. But this soon disappeared as he was given a 25-second penalty for passing the Sauber of Nick Heidfeld under yellow flags. And so Heidfeld was elevated to fourth, Frentzen to fifth and Kimi Räikkönen to sixth on his Grand Prix debut in the second Sauber, not bad for someone starting only the 24th race of his career since stepping up from karts.

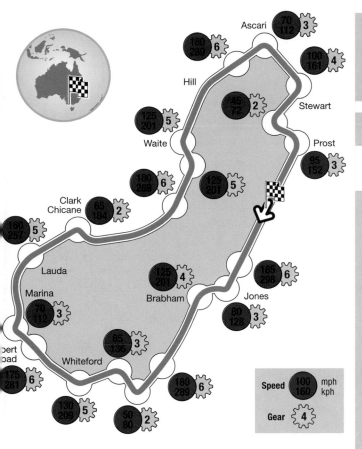

Ascari 70 112 **3** 180 289 **6**
100 161 **4**
Hill
45 72 **2** **Stewart**
125 201 **5**
Waite **Prost**
95 152 **3**
180 289 **6** 125 201 **5**
Clark Chicane 65 104 **2**
180 257 **5**
185 298 **6**
Lauda 125 201 **4**
Marina 70 112 **3** **Brabham** **Jones**
80 128 **3**
85 136 **3**
175 281 **6** bert oad
Whiteford 180 289 **6**
130 209 **5** 50 80 **2**

Speed 100 160 mph kph
Gear 4

Pole time
Michael Schumacher, 1m 26.892s, 136.526mph / 219.670kph

Winner's average speed
116.490mph / 187.432kph

Fastest lap
Michael Schumacher, 1m 28.214s, 134.480mph / 216.378kph

Lap leaders
M Schumacher, 1–36, 41–58; Coulthard, 37–40

And He's Off: Michael Schumacher blasts into an immediate lead

 MELBOURNE ROUND 1

Date 4 March 2001 **Laps** 58 **Distance** 191.57 miles / 308.24 km
Weather Warm, dry and bright

RACE RESULTS

Position	Driver	Team	Result	Stops	Qualify Time	Grid
1	**Michael Schumacher**	Ferrari	1h 38m 26.533s	1	1m 26.892s	1
2	**David Coulthard**	McLaren	1h 38m 28.251s	1	1m 28.010s	6
3	**Rubens Barrichello**	Ferrari	1h 39m 00.024s	1	1m 27.263s	2
4	**Nick Heidfeld**	Sauber	1h 39m 38.012s	1	1m 28.615s	10
5	**Heinz-Harald Frentzen**	Jordan	1h 39m 39.340s	1	1m 27.658s	4
6	**Kimi Räikkönen**	Sauber	1h 39m 50.676s	1	1m 28.993s	13
7	**Olivier Panis**	BAR	1h 39m 53.583s*	1	1m 28.518s	9
8	**Luciano Burti**	Jaguar	57 laps	1	1m 30.978s	21
9	**Jean Alesi**	Prost	57 laps	1	1m 29.893s	14
10	**Jos Verstappen**	Arrows	57 laps*	2	1m 29.934s	15
11	**Eddie Irvine**	Jaguar	57 laps	1	1m 28.965s	12
12	**Fernando Alonso**	Minardi	56 laps	2	1m 30.657s	19
13	**Giancarlo Fisichella**	Benetton	55 laps	2	1m 30.209s	17
14	**Jenson Button**	Benetton	52 laps	2	1m 30.035s	16
R	**Juan Pablo Montoya**	Williams	engine	-	1m 28.738s	11
R	**Jarno Trulli**	Jordan	engine	1	1m 28.377s	7
R	**Mika Hakkinen**	McLaren	suspension	-	1m 27.461s	3
R	**Ralf Schumacher**	Williams	accident	-	1m 27.719s	5
R	**Jacques Villeneuve**	BAR	accident	-	1m 28.435s	8
R	**Tarso Marques**	Minardi	battery	-	1m 33.228s	22
R	**Enrique Bernoldi**	Arrows	accident	-	1m 30.520s	18
R	**Gaston Mazzacane**	Prost	brake pedal	-	1m 30.798s	20

* Penalised 25 seconds for overtaking under yellow flags

MALAYSIAN GP

MICHAEL IN A MONSOON

When it's wet, it takes a brave person to bet against anyone other than Michael Schumacher taking victory. And so it was that he made it two victories from two starts, leading home Rubens Barrichello for a Ferrari one-two at Sepang.

Michael Schumacher made it six wins in a row when he dominated proceedings at Sepang. Amazingly, though, he and Ferrari team-mate Rubens Barrichello ran as low as 10th and 11th in the early stages before staggering onlookers as they lapped at up to six seconds faster than their leading rivals.

That's jumping ahead a little, though. For, after surviving a clash with Ralf Schumacher at the first corner of the opening lap, Barrichello tucked in behind race leader Michael. However, they didn't run first and second for long as both hit oil dropped by Olivier Panis's exploding Honda engine, and slid off the track for a ride over grass and gravel before rejoining.

Their bacon was saved, however, as it was on this very lap that rain started to fall – and fall hard. Cars began to spin off all around the circuit, with Jarno Trulli skating out of the lead at the final corner. David Coulthard then assumed the lead and promptly spun before pitting. With the Safety Car called onto the soaking track, Coulthard emerged from the pits at the head of the

MEMORABLE MOMENT

Having hosted only three Grands Prix, the choice for an outstanding race is limited. However, the early laps of last year's race will remain with those who watched them. Rain always affects races, but what fell at Sepang was a deluge, and car after car spun off the track. First the Ferraris ran wide on oil, then the skies opened and Jarno Trulli took over, but he also spun. Behind him, David Coulthard did the same and the Safety Car was scrambled, but already five cars were out for the day.

train. Ferrari's pit stops are the stuff of legends, but this time it went wrong as the team were caught out by Barrichello coming around ahead of Schumacher. They had Michael's tyres ready for Rubens, and none ready at all for Michael, who had to sit patiently behind waiting for his turn. They both rejoined eventually to run 10th and 11th, but they had had some good fortune as their guess that the soaring temperatures would soon dry the track out proved correct and they alone had fitted intermediate tyres rather than full wets, and the intermediate tyres proved to be the ones to have.

Thus Schumacher and Barrichello ripped their way through the field, hitting the front on lap 16, having just passed Jos Verstappen, who was enjoying some rare moments of glory for Arrows. Barrichello lost time with an early second stop to clear his sidepods of debris, but still had enough in hand to keep Coulthard back in third.

With Verstappen needing two more stops, Ralf Schumacher climbed to fourth after a strong recovery from his first-corner spin. He too was to pit three times, however, and so Heinz-Harald Frentzen raced on to fourth ahead of Ralf and an off-the-pace Mika Hakkinen.

Panic Stations: A sudden deluge in the early laps led to a rush of hurried tyre-changing

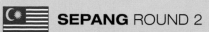

Speed **100** mph / **160** kph

Gear **4**

SEPANG ROUND 2

Date 18 March 2001 **Laps** 55 **Distance** 189.44 miles / 304.81 km
Weather Very hot and humid then heavy rain, drying later

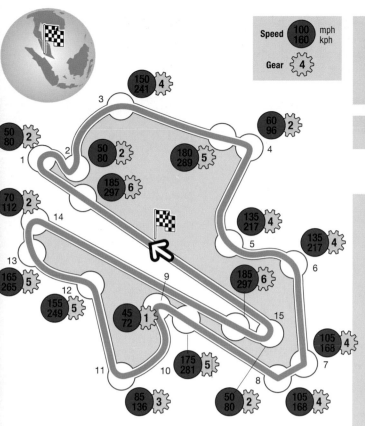

| 150 | 4 |
| 241 | |

| 60 | 2 |
| 96 | |

| 50 | 2 |
| 80 | |

| 50 | 2 |
| 80 | |

| 180 | 5 |
| 289 | |

| 185 | 6 |
| 297 | |

| 70 | 2 |
| 112 | |

| 135 | 4 |
| 217 | |

| 135 | 4 |
| 217 | |

| 165 | 5 |
| 265 | |

| 185 | 6 |
| 297 | |

| 155 | 5 |
| 249 | |

| 45 | 1 |
| 72 | |

| 105 | 4 |
| 168 | |

| 175 | 5 |
| 281 | |

| 85 | 3 |
| 136 | |

| 50 | 2 |
| 80 | |

| 105 | 4 |
| 168 | |

RACE RESULTS

Position	Driver	Team	Result	Stops	Qualify Time	Grid
1	Michael Schumacher	Ferrari	1h 47m 34.801s	2	1m 35.220s	1
2	Rubens Barrichello	Ferrari	1h 47m 58.461s	2	1m 35.319s	2
3	David Coulthard	McLaren	1h 48m 03.356s	2	1m 36.417s	8
4	Heinz-Harald Frentzen	Jordan	1h 48m 21.344s	2	1m 36.578s	9
5	Ralf Schumacher	Williams	1h 48m 23.034s	3	1m 35.511s	3
6	Mika Hakkinen	McLaren	1h 48m 23.407s	3	1m 36.040s	4
7	Jos Verstappen	Arrows	1h 48m 56.361s	3	1m 38.509s	18
8	Jarno Trulli	Jordan	54 laps	2	1m 36.180s	5
9	Jean Alesi	Prost	54 laps	2	1m 37.406s	13
10	Luciano Burti	Jaguar	54 laps	2	1m 38.035s	15
11	Jenson Button	Benetton	53 laps	2	1m 38.258s	17
12	Gaston Mazzacane	Prost	53 laps	3	1m 39.006s	19
13	Fernando Alonso	Minardi	52 laps	5	1m 40.249s	21
14	Tarso Marques	Minardi	51 laps	2	1m 39.714s	20
R	Giancarlo Fisichella	Benetton	oil pump	2	1m 38.086s	16
R	Jacques Villeneuve	BAR	spun off	0	1m 36.397s	7
R	Nick Heidfeld	Sauber	spun off	0	1m 36.913s	11
R	Enrique Bernoldi	Arrows	spun off	0	no time*	22
R	Juan Pablo Montoya	Williams	spun off	0	1m 36.218s	6
R	Eddie Irvine	Jaguar	crash damage	0	1m 37.140s	12
R	Olivier Panis	BAR	oil pump	0	1m 36.681s	10
R	Kimi Räikkönen	Sauber	transmission	0	1m 37.728s	14

* Qualifying result of 1m 38.708s annulled for front-wing irregularity

Pole time

Michael Schumacher, 1m 35.220s, 130.224mph / 209.530kph

Winner's average speed

105.657mph / 170.002kph

Fastest lap

Mika Hakkinen, 1m 40.962s, 122.817mph / 197.613kph

Lap leaders

M Schumacher, 1–2, 16–55; Trulli, 3; Coulthard, 4–15

Red Attack: Jordan's Jarno Trulli has his mirrors full of red as Ferrari's
Michael Schumacher and Rubens Barrichello prepare to blast past

BRAZILIAN GP

SOMETHING FOR EVERYONE

Not only did the Brazilian GP bring Michael Schumacher's six-race winning streak to a close, but it offered fans the chance to see Juan Pablo Montoya lead for the first time – as well as thrills and spills before, during and after the rain swept in – and the sight of Coulthard sweeping around Schumacher before going on to score his first win of 2001.

Mika Hakkinen stalled at the start and had to endure the pack squeezing past on either side on this narrow grid hemmed in by walls. The Safety Car was deployed so that Hakkinen's McLaren could be removed and it was when it withdrew that Juan Pablo Montoya struck. He was behind Michael Schumacher, but used his knowledge of restarts gained in Champ Car racing. Harnessing the massive horsepower of his BMW engine on the climb to the start/finish straight, he dived down the inside into the first corner. Schumacher tried to block him but then realised that Montoya wasn't backing off, and they entered the corner side-by-side. Montoya edged Schumacher toward the grass so he had to lift off the throttle. The king had been beaten.

Montoya settled into the lead, with Schumacher unable to mount a challenge. Amazingly, it was later revealed that the Ferrari was on a planned two-stop strategy, while the Williams was carrying 40kg more fuel and planning to stop only once. David Coulthard held a watching brief behind them as Ralf Schumacher and Rubens Barrichello both limped back to the pits after a collision.

When Schumacher brought his Ferrari in for the first of his planned stops, Coulthard moved into second, but there was nothing he

76

REVIEW OF 2001

MEMORABLE MOMENT

Interlagos has hosted some fabulous races, but the one in 1991 stands out both for the race itself and for the delirious celebration that followed Ayrton Senna winning his home grand prix at the eighth attempt. With 27 wins under his belt, it had to come. Sure, he led from start to finish, but he was never allowed to let up as his McLaren was pushed by the Williams duo of Nigel Mansell then Riccardo Patrese, with drama being added when his gearbox started to lose gears. For the final lap, he stuck it in sixth gear and kept it there. So great was Ayrton's effort that he had to be lifted from the car.

could do about Montoya. However, he didn't have to, as Montoya was hit from behind by Jos Verstappen after he lapped the Dutchman's Arrows. Coulthard pitted and returned in the lead.

Half-a-dozen laps later, rain began to fall. This looked to be to Schumacher's benefit, as he was due to pit again soon. On went the intermediates, as Coulthard slithered around for a further lap before pitting for similar rubber. However, the Scot's car had started on a semi-wet set-up, while Michael's was full-dry. Using this to his advantage, Coulthard closed in. Two laps later, he pulled off a magnificent move into the first corner as Schumacher went around the outside of backmarker Tarso Marques, and Coulthard passed both of them down the inside. Coulthard then powered clear for his first win since July 2000.

Third place, a lap down, went to Nick Heidfeld, passing Heinz-Harald Frentzen whose engine failed in the closing laps. Olivier Panis, Jarno Trulli and Giancarlo Fisichella claimed the minor points, while Jean Alesi lost out after being delayed by a refuelling rig that refused to pour.

In Control: David Coulthard dived past Michael Schumacher for his first win of 2001

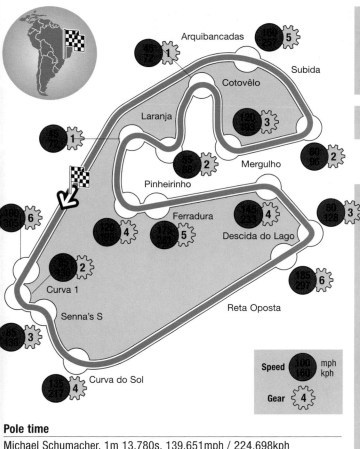

Arquibancadas

Subida

Cotovêlo

Laranja

Mergulho

Pinheirinho

Ferradura

Descida do Lago

Curva 1

Senna's S

Reta Oposta

Curva do Sol

Speed	100 mph / 160 kph
Gear	4

Pole time
Michael Schumacher, 1m 13.780s, 139.651mph / 224.698kph

Winner's average speed
115.191mph / 185.342kph

Fastest lap
Ralf Schumacher, 1m 15.693s, 127.348mph / 204.903kph

Lap leaders
M Schumacher, 1–2, 48–49; Montoya, 3–38; Coulthard, 39–47, 50–71

Here I Come: Montoya throws down a challenge to champion Schumacher

INTERLAGOS ROUND 3

Date 1 April 2001 **Laps** 71 **Distance** 190.09 miles / 305.85 km
Weather Hot and sunny, raining mid-race then drying

RACE RESULTS

Position	Driver	Team	Result	Stops	Qualify Time	Grid
1	David Coulthard	McLaren	1h 39m 00.834s	2	1m 14.178s	5
2	Michael Schumacher	Ferrari	1h 39m 16.998s	2	1m 13.780s	1
3	Nick Heidfeld	Sauber	70 laps	1	1m 14.810s	9
4	Olivier Panis	BAR	70 laps	2	1m 15.046s	11
5	Jarno Trulli	Jordan	70 laps	1	1m 14.630s	7
6	Giancarlo Fisichella	Benetton	70 laps	2	1m 16.175s	18
7	Jacques Villeneuve	BAR	70 laps	2	1m 15.182s	12
8	Jean Alesi	Prost	70 laps	2	1m 15.437s	15
9	Tarso Marques	Minardi	68 laps	2	1m 16.784s	22
10	Jenson Button	Benetton	64 laps	2	1m 16.229s	20
11	Heinz-Harald Frentzen	Jordan	63 laps	2	1m 14.633s	8
R	Kimi Räikkönen	Sauber	spun off	2	1m 14.924s	10
R	Gaston Mazzacane	Prost	clutch	2	1m 16.520s	21
R	Ralf Schumacher	Williams	spun off	2	1m 14.090s	2
R	Eddie Irvine	Jaguar	spun off	2	1m 15.192s	13
R	Juan Pablo Montoya	Williams	accident	0	1m 14.165s	4
R	Jos Verstappen	Arrows	accident	0	1m 15.704s	17
R	Luciano Burti	Jaguar	water seal	0	1m 15.371s	14
R	Fernando Alonso	Minardi	throttle	0	1m 16.184s	19
R	Enrique Bernoldi	Arrows	hydraulics	0	1m 15.657s	16
R	Rubens Barrichello	Ferrari	accident	0	1m 14.191s	6
R	Mika Hakkinen	McLaren	clutch	0	1m 14.122s	3

SAN MARINO GP

RALF'S FIRST FIRST

Not only did Ralf Schumacher score his first Grand Prix victory, but he did so by leading every lap in a faultless drive that saw his Williams outpace the McLarens and Ferraris. It was also Michelin's first win since their return to Formula One.

All a Blur: Jarno Trulli was very quick at the lights, even beating Michael Schumacher away

MEMORABLE MOMENT

Only 14 cars turned up for the 1982 San Marino GP, and only Ferrari and Renault were competitive. However, it remains a seminal race, remembered for the jousting between Gilles Villeneuve and Didier Pironi that appeared to be stage-managed but which turned nasty when team orders were ignored. With both Renaults having retired, the Ferrari drivers traded places. Then, when instructed to hold station, Pironi helped himself to victory on the final lap. Villeneuve never spoke to his former friend again, and died at the next Grand Prix when trying to outqualify him.

Springtime in Italy usually means warm days beneath gentle sunshine. Not last year, though, with snow falling but not settling in the surrounding hills when the drivers ventured out for the Saturday morning practice sessions. And this revealed that Michelin didn't have a tyre that could perform when it was both cold and wet. Indeed, at one stage the fastest driver using their tyres, Ralf Schumacher, was eight seconds off the pace. This was reduced to just over two seconds, but even that is the difference between night and day in Formula One. However, the sun came out and Ralf scorched his Williams around to third on the grid in qualifying that lunchtime – behind only the McLarens – with brother Michael's Ferrari fourth fastest.

At the start, Ralf was fastest away and ran briefly on the grass as he blasted past polesitter David Coulthard to take the lead. Although the Scot tucked in behind, he was unable to do anything about Schumacher. His Finnish team-mate was enjoying his outing even less as he was demoted by Jarno Trulli, whose Jordan had been faster away at the start than Michael Schumacher's Ferrari. This was to prove a problem for those behind, as Trulli was unable to match the pace of Ralf and David, letting them escape as those behind fumed.

Using the obvious straightline speed of his BMW engine to good effect, Juan Pablo Montoya demoted Michael Schumacher to take fifth on lap 3. The German was having to cope with a gearshift problem, but this became irrelevant when a brake duct came loose and damaged a wheel rim, leading to his retirement. Already gone from the train of cars behind him was Kimi Räikkönen, who impressed in no small measure before his steering wheel came off and he crashed.

Running a long first stint, Rubens Barrichello was able to move ahead of Hakkinen for third. Montoya hoped to do likewise, after passing Trulli, but his gearbox became jammed in first as he left the pits and that was that. The minor places were then sorted as the two Jordans, both lapped, rounded out the top six.

The day belonged, though, to BMW, Michelin and Ralf Schumacher, with Ralf making the Schumachers the first brothers to win in Formula One.

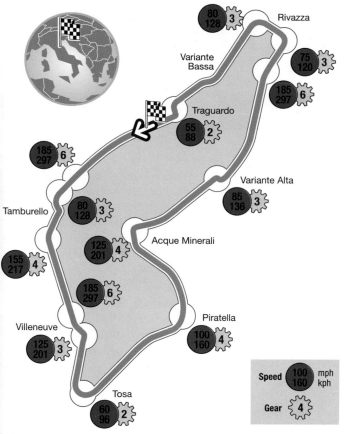

Rivazza

80
128 | 3

Variante
Bassa

75
120 | 3

185
297 | 6

Traguardo

55
88 | 2

185
297 | 6

Variante Alta

Tamburello

80
128 | 3

85
136 | 3

125
201 | 4

Acque Minerali

155
217 | 4

185
297 | 6

Piratella

Villeneuve

100
160 | 4

125
201 | 3

Speed	100 / 160	mph / kph
Gear	4	

Tosa

60
96 | 2

Pole time
David Coulthard, 1m 23.054s, 132.869mph / 213.786kph

Winner's average speed
125.561mph / 202.028kph

Fastest lap
Ralf Schumacher, 1m 25.524s, 129.031mph / 207.611kph

Lap leaders
R Schumacher, 1–62

A Flying Start: Ralf Schumacher hit the front and stayed there

 IMOLA ROUND 4

Date 15 April 2001 **Laps** 62 **Distance** 189.91 miles / 305.56 km
Weather Cool, dry and bright

RACE RESULTS

Position	Driver	Team	Result	Stops	Qualify Time	Grid
1	Ralf Schumacher	Williams	1h 30m 44.817s	2	1m 23.357s	3
2	David Coulthard	McLaren	1h 30m 49.169s	2	1m 23.054s	1
3	Rubens Barrichello	Ferrari	1h 31m 19.583s	2	1m 23.786s	6
4	Mika Hakkinen	McLaren	1h 31m 21.132s	2	1m 23.282s	2
5	Jarno Trulli	Jordan	1h 32m 10.375s	2	1m 23.658s	5
6	Heinz-Harald Frentzen	Jordan	61 laps	2	1m 24.436s	9
7	Nick Heidfeld	Sauber	61 laps	2	1m 25.007s	12
8	Olivier Panis	BAR	61 laps	2	1m 24.213s	8
9	Jean Alesi	Prost	61 laps	2	1m 25.411s	14
10	Enrique Bernoldi	Arrows	60 laps	2	1m 25.872s	16
11	Luciano Burti	Jaguar	60 laps	1	1m 25.572s	15
12	Jenson Button	Benetton	60 laps	3	1m 27.758s	21
R	Tarso Marques	Minardi	engine	2	1m 28.281s	22
R	Juan Pablo Montoya	Williams	clutch	2	1m 24.141s	7
R	Eddie Irvine	Jaguar	engine	1	1m 25.392s	13
R	Giancarlo Fisichella	Benetton	misfire	1	1m 26.902s	19
R	Jacques Villeneuve	BAR	engine	1	1m 24.769s	11
R	Gaston Mazzacane	Prost	engine	1	1m 27.750s	20
R	Michael Schumacher	Ferrari	withdrew	1	1m 23.593s	4
R	Kimi Räikkönen	Sauber	steering wheel	0	1m 24.671s	10
R	Jos Verstappen	Arrows	exhaust	0	1m 26.062s	17
R	Fernando Alonso	Minardi	accident	0	1m 26.855s	18

SPANISH GP

WOE IS MIKA

Just when Mika Hakkinen thought that his unrewarding start to the season couldn't get any worse, it did. Heading for a clear victory, with just half a lap to go, his clutch exploded – handing a surprise win back to Michael Schumacher, whose Ferrari had slowed with tyre vibration.

MEMORABLE MOMENT

Ayrton Senna featured in many memorable moments, but one of the most exciting was the 1991 Spanish GP. This was the first race at the new Circuit de Catalunya, north of Barcelona, and it was held amid a sea of accusations about driving standards. His chief rival Nigel Mansell had made a slow start, but put his Williams in the McLaren's slipstream down the long main straight on lap 5, and onlookers winced as they came close to touching several times at 190mph (306kph) as neither gave ground on the approach to the first corner. Mansell got through, but it was a powerplay of the clearest order.

This was the race that marked the arrival of traction control and launch control as legal ingredients, and their arrival wasn't without problems, with David Coulthard stalling at the start of the parade lap and then Heinz-Harald Frentzen failing to get away at all at the start.

If McLaren thought that Coulthard had used up its quota of bad luck when he was forced him to start from the back of the grid, they were wrong. Indeed, caught up in first-corner turmoil, he had his car's nose wing knocked off and pitted for another, making even a handful of points unlikely. But Lady Luck deserted Hakkinen on the closing lap just as he was dreaming of his first win since the Belgian GP in August 2000.

To get into the position of leading by 40 seconds with less than two miles to go, Mika ran longer stints than Michael Schumacher, taking over when the German came in for his second stop. Then, on his third set of tyres, Michael slowed with a worrying vibration. There were concerns that he'd been told to

Still Stunned: Hakkinen arrives back at parc fermé on team-mate Coulthard's sidepod

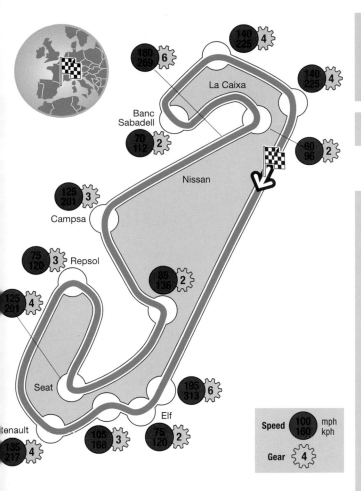

CIRCUIT DE CATALUNYA ROUND 5

Date 29 April 2001 **Laps** 65 **Distance** 190.97 miles / 307.27 km
Weather Warm but overcast

RACE RESULTS

Position	Driver	Team	Result	Stops	Qualify Time	Grid
1	Michael Schumacher	Ferrari	1h 31m 03.305s	2	1m 18.201s	1
2	Juan Pablo Montoya	Williams	1h 31m 44.042s	2	1m 19.660s	12
3	Jacques Villeneuve	BAR	1h 31m 52.930s	2	1m 19.122s	7
4	Jarno Trulli	Jordan	1h 31m 54.557s	2	1m 19.093s	6
5	David Coulthard	McLaren	1h 31m 54.920s	3	1m 18.635s	3
6	Nick Heidfeld	Sauber	1h 32m 05.197s	2	1m 19.232s	10
7	Olivier Panis	BAR	1h 32m 08.281s	2	1m 19.479s	11
8	Kimi Räikkönen	Sauber	1h 32m 23.112s	2	1m 19.229s	9
9	Mika Hakkinen	McLaren	64 laps	2	1m 18.286s	2
10	Jean Alesi	Prost	64 laps	2	1m 20.601s	15
11	Luciano Burti	Prost	64 laps	2	1m 20.585s	14
12	Jos Verstappen	Arrows	63 laps	2	1m 20.737s	17
13	Fernando Alonso	Minardi	63 laps	2	1m 21.037s	18
14	Giancarlo Fisichella	Benetton	63 laps	2	1m 21.065s	19
15	Jenson Button	Benetton	62 laps	2	1m 21.916s	21
16	Tarso Marques	Minardi	62 laps	2	1m 22.522s	22
R	Rubens Barrichello	Ferrari	suspension	3	1m 18.674s	4
R	Eddie Irvine	Jaguar	engine	2	1m 20.326s	13
R	Ralf Schumacher	Williams	spun off	0	1m 19.016s	5
R	Enrique Bernoldi	Arrows	engine	0	1m 20.696s	16
R	Pedro de la Rosa	Jaguar	accident	0	1m 21.338s	20
R	Heinz-Harald Frentzen	Jordan	accident	0	1m 19.150s	8

Pole time
Michael Schumacher, 1m 18.201s, 135.289mph / 217.68kph

Winner's average speed
125.838mph / 202.473kph

Fastest lap
Michael Schumacher, 1m 21.151s, 130.389mph / 209.796kph

Lap leaders
M Schumacher, 1–22, 28–43, 65; Hakkinen, 23–27, 44–64

slow by the team after team-mate Rubens Barrichello retired with rear suspension failure, but post-race analysis revealed that his tyres were turning on their rims. Michael kept going and was still well clear of Juan Pablo Montoya's Williams for his third win in the first five races. It's not often that Michael looks bashful, but he didn't know what to do with himself when he took the chequered flag. In gentlemanly form, he immediately sought out Hakkinen in parc fermé and offered his commiserations.

While Montoya was ecstatic to be on the podium for the first time, Jacques Villeneuve was also pleased to be there, as it was the first time that he had done so for BAR. Dead last after having a new nose fitted, Coulthard was eighth when he made his first regular stop and sixth by his second. Hakkinen's retirement elevated him to fifth at the flag, hot on the tail of Villeneuve and Jarno Trulli, but it only served to emphasize that if he'd been able to start from the second row, then he would probably have won.

Although Montoya and Villeneuve had reason to smile, Jaguar's personnel had long faces as Eddie Irvine's best drive of the year was scuppered by engine failure.

Midfield Men: Jean Alesi did the best he could for Prost, but was still lapped. Jarno Trulli raced to his equal best finish of 2001 for Jordan, fourth

AUSTRIAN GP

COULTHARD'S WINNING TACTICS

David Coulthard put his title challenge back on track with a tactical victory. But it is for the team orders that forced Rubens Barrichello to pull over on the final lap to let Ferrari team-mate Michael Schumacher through to second that the race will be remembered.

When McLaren's cars lined up seventh and eighth after a loss of form in qualifying, Michael Schumacher must have been rubbing his hands with glee. Although he was sure they would perform better in the race, they would have to pass six cars to get to him. Instead, the three-time World Champion was more worried about reaching the tight first corner in front of the two Williams cars that were lining up second and third. As it happened, Michael's launch control didn't work well, and by the time he had switched to a manual getaway he was third, with Juan Pablo Montoya leading Michael's brother Ralf.

At least he got away, though, which is more than can be said of four of the 22 drivers, as Jordan's Jarno Trulli and Heinz-Harald Frentzen were left stationary in fifth and eleventh, Nick Heidfeld's Sauber in sixth and Mika Hakkinen's McLaren in eighth. Mercifully, everyone managed to avoid them, but it spelled another race without points for the frustrated Hakkinen.

Williams's hopes of a one-two were thwarted when Ralf Schumacher's brakes

82

REVIEW OF 2001

MEMORABLE MOMENT

The circuit has had its moments as the A1-Ring, but it was in its previous incarnation as the Osterreichring that it had its greatest moment. This came in the closing laps of the 1982 Austrian GP after runaway leader Alain Prost had parked his Renault as Keke Rosberg, desperate for his first win, hunted down Elio de Angelis. The Williams got closer and closer to the now misfiring Lotus, but the Italian resisted all, blocked Rosberg through the final corner and held on to score his first win, the closest ever margin of victory at just 0.05 seconds. Rosberg was to win next time out, at Dijon-Prenois.

failed, and so Michael moved on to Montoya's tail. Perhaps reckoning that the Michelin tyres might go off, he bided his time, as Rubens Barrichello, Jos Verstappen (flying with a light fuel load), Coulthard and Kimi Räikkönen ran in line astern.

Then Michael made a move around the outside of Montoya and the Colombian elected not to cede, but he was unable to complete his braking in time, putting both of them on the grass and dropping them to sixth and seventh respectively. So it was that Barrichello took the lead, and Coulthard advanced to second when Verstappen came in for the first of his two stops. The others would be pitting only once, and it was the fact that Coulthard came in last of all and thus would be putting in the least amount of fuel that meant that he emerged in the lead.

The remaining laps of the race had Barrichello sitting on his tail, with Michael closing in behind. The Brazilian was furious when the call came from Jean Todt, but as Ferrari number two he knew that it was in his contract and grudgingly pulled over on the final sprint to the line to let Michael through for second.

Early Running: Montoya leads from Schumacher, Barrichello, Verstappen and Coulthard

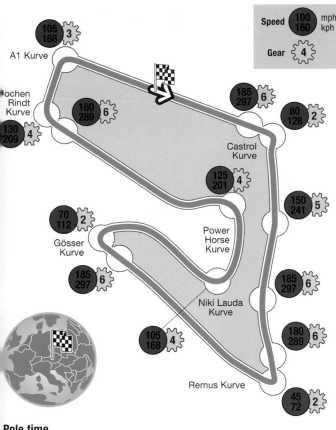

Speed 100 mph / 160 kph
Gear 4

A1 Kurve — 105 / 168 — 3
Jochen Rindt Kurve — 180 / 289 — 6
130 / 209 — 4
Castrol Kurve — 185 / 297 — 6
80 / 128 — 2
125 / 201 — 4
150 / 241 — 5
Power Horse Kurve
70 / 112 — 2
Gösser Kurve
185 / 297 — 6
185 / 297 — 6
Niki Lauda Kurve
105 / 168 — 4
180 / 289 — 6
Remus Kurve
45 / 72 — 2

Pole time
Michael Schumacher, 1m 09.562s, 139.119mph / 223.842kph

Winner's average speed
130.480mph / 209.942kph

Fastest lap
David Coulthard, 1m 10.843s, 136.604mph / 219.796kph

Lap leaders
Montoya, 1–15; Barrichello, 16–46; Coulthard, 47–71

Tactical Masterstroke: Coulthard's late stop put him into the lead

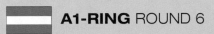

A1-RING ROUND 6

Date 13 May 2001 **Laps** 71 **Distance** 190.86 miles / 307.09 km
Weather Warm, dry and bright

RACE RESULTS

Position	Driver	Team	Result	Stops	Qualify Time	Grid
1	David Coulthard	McLaren	1h 27m 45.927s	1	1m 10.331s	7
2	Michael Schumacher	Ferrari	1h 27m 48.117s	1	1m 09.786s	4
3	Rubens Barrichello	Ferrari	1h 27m 48.454s	1	1m 09.562s	1
4	Kimi Räikkönen	Sauber	1h 28m 27.520s	1	1m 10.396s	9
5	Olivier Panis	BAR	1h 28m 39.702s	1	1m 10.435s	10
6	Jos Verstappen	Arrows	70 laps	2	1m 12.187s	16
7	Eddie Irvine	Jaguar	70 laps	1	1m 11.632s	13
8	Jacques Villeneuve	BAR	70 laps	1	1m 11.058s	12
9	Nick Heidfeld	Sauber	69 laps	1	1m 10.211s	6
10	Jean Alesi	Prost	69 laps	1	1m 12.910s	20
11	Luciano Burti	Prost	69 laps	1	1m 12.206s	17
R	Jenson Button	Benetton	engine	1	1m 13.459s	21
R	Pedro de la Rosa	Jaguar	transmission	1	1m 11.752s	14
R	Juan Pablo Montoya	Williams	hydraulics	0	1m 09.686s	2
R	Fernando Alonso	Minardi	gearbox	0	1m 12.640s	18
R	Tarso Marques	Minardi	gearbox	0	1m 13.585s	22
R	Enrique Bernoldi	Arrows	hydraulics	0	1m 11.823s	15
DQ	Jarno Trulli	Jordan	pit infringement	0	1m 10.202s	5
R	Ralf Schumacher	Williams	brakes	0	1m 09.760s	3
R	Giancarlo Fisichella	Benetton	engine	0	1m 12.644s	19
R	Mika Hakkinen	McLaren	electronics	0	1m 10.342s	8
R	Heinz-Harald Frentzen	Jordan	gearbox	0	1m 10.923s	11

MONACO GP

SCHUMI BACK IN FRONT

Michael Schumacher was given a gift when pole-sitter David Coulthard's launch control failed and forced the Scot to start from the back of the grid. With overtaking all but impossible here, the Ferrari ace was left to win as he pleased.

Cat Gets the Cream: Eddie Irvine guides his Jaguar to a surprise third place behind the Ferraris

MEMORABLE MOMENT

The 1982 Monaco GP stands out from all others, but this was for a final flurry, whereas the 1961 race was a thriller from start to finish. In this, the first race of the 1.5-litre formula, Ferrari's Richie Ginther led away but Stirling Moss stuck with him in his privately-entered Lotus. He soon led, chased now by Porsche's Jo Bonnier, but the Ferraris fought back, with Phil Hill and Ginther closing in. The cars that were to dominate the season were clearly faster, but Moss used all his guile to stay ahead and beat Ginther to the flag by just three seconds after 100 laps.

With four of the 22 cars having stalled on the grid at the previous race, there was concern that there could be trouble on Monaco's narrow grid. However, despite David Coulthard having stalled in Spain and Mika Hakkinen in Austria, McLaren was confident, especially as Coulthard had produced a blinding lap to usurp Michael Schumacher from pole. Unfortunately, he had to start from the back of the grid, as when he pressed his launch control button at the start of the parade lap, his engine cut out.

Schumacher made the most of his new-found "pole" and pulled away from Hakkinen and Rubens Barrichello as he pleased, while Coulthard was immediately aware that despite having the potential to be the fastest driver, there was little he could do if the driver ahead of him didn't want to let him past. After passing Tarso Marques, he found himself stuck behind Enrique Bernoldi's Arrows. And there he stayed as the Brazilian closed the door on every move. Bernoldi felt that he was fighting for position and wouldn't yield. McLaren boss Ron Dennis felt that Bernoldi should let his World Championship challenger through, but Arrows boss Tom Walkinshaw told Bernoldi to stay where he was. McLaren's woes increased when

Hakkinen retired from second because his car was pulling to one side.

When Schumacher and his chasers came up to lap Coulthard, David pulled aside to let them through but was never able to nip past Bernoldi in the same move as Schumacher and others dived past. He would have to wait until Bernoldi pitted, which he did on lap 43, with Coulthard immediately lapping four seconds faster. Coulthard stayed out for a further 22 laps, thanks to his car's larger-than-average fuel-tank size, and thanks also to having leaned off his fuel mixture while stuck behind Bernoldi. He rejoined in sixth, and this became fifth when Jean Alesi pitted with a puncture.

On Hakkinen's departure from the race, Barrichello advanced to second and Ralf Schumacher to third, but the German was not to last the race, his car's electrics failing. This left Eddie Irvine finally to give Jaguar something to smile about as he held off Jacques Villeneuve's BAR to improve on Jaguar's previous best result, his fourth at Monaco in 2000. A lap down, Coulthard was rewarded with two points for his perseverance, with Alesi delighted to get Prost into the points with sixth place.

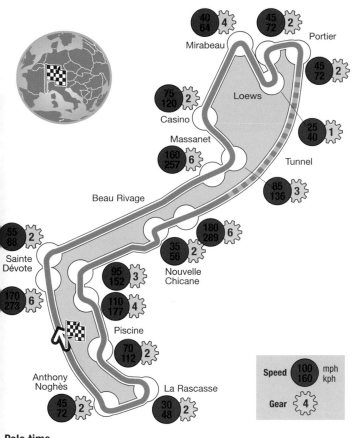

 MONTE CARLO ROUND 7

Date 27 May 2001 **Laps** 78 **Distance** 163.34 miles / 262.81 km
Weather Warm, dry and bright

RACE RESULTS

Position	Driver	Team	Result	Stops	Qualify Time	Grid
1	Michael Schumacher	Ferrari	1h 47m 22.561s	1	1m 17.631s	2
2	Rubens Barrichello	Ferrari	1h 47m 22.992s	1	1m 17.856s	4
3	Eddie Irvine	Jaguar	1h 47m 53.259s	1	1m 18.432s	6
4	Jacques Villeneuve	BAR	1h 47m 55.015s	1	1m 19.086s	9
5	David Coulthard	McLaren	77 laps	1	1m 17.430s	1
6	Jean Alesi	Prost	77 laps	2	1m 19.245s	11
7	Jenson Button	Benetton	77 laps	1	1m 20.342s	17
8	Jos Verstappen	Arrows	77 laps	1	1m 20.823s	19
9	Enrique Bernoldi	Arrows	76 laps	1	1m 21.336s	20
10	Kimi Räikkönen	Sauber	73 laps	2	1m 20.081s	15
R	Ralf Schumacher	Williams	hydraulics	0	1m 18.029s	5
R	Tarso Marques	Minardi	driveshaft	1	1m 22.201s	22
R	Fernando Alonso	Minardi	gearbox	1	1m 20.788s	18
R	Heinz-Harald Frentzen	Jordan	accident	0	1m 19.316s	13
R	Giancarlo Fisichella	Benetton	accident	0	1m 19.220s	10
R	Jarno Trulli	Jordan	engine	0	1m 18.921s	8
R	Luciano Burti	Prost	gearbox	1	1m 21.771s	21
R	Pedro de la Rosa	Jaguar	gearbox	0	1m 20.033s	14
R	Mika Hakkinen	McLaren	suspension	1	1m 17.749s	3
R	Olivier Panis	BAR	steering	2	1m 19.294s	12
R	Juan Pablo Montoya	Williams	accident	0	1m 18.751s	7
R	Nick Heidfeld	Sauber	accident	0	1m 20.261s	16

Pole time
David Coulthard, 1m 17.430s, 97.363mph / 156.657kph

Winner's average speed
91.272mph / 146.857kph

Fastest lap
David Coulthard, 1m 19.424s, 94.918mph / 152.723kph

Lap leaders
M Schumacher, 1–54, 60–78; Barrichello, 55–59

No Luck: Despite scorching to pole, Coulthard had to start from the back

CANADIAN GP

MOVE OVER, BROTHER

The Schumachers claimed the first ever Formula One one-two result by a pair of brothers, with Ralf biding his time before putting one over his older sibling Michael as Williams again showed its supremacy.

There was drama as the cars assembled on the grid to wait for the red lights to come on, with Coulthard throwing something over the pitwall to his crew. It turns out that this was a nut that he'd found loose in his McLaren's cockpit. But then the lights went out and the Scot tucked into third as the front-row-starting Schumachers fought for position into the first corner. Ralf challenged Michael but had to cede.

Unusually, everyone filed through the tricky first-corner complex, but already McLaren knew that Coulthard would be having a torrid time as the nut that he'd thrown to them

proved to be from his car's front suspension. However, despite worsening handling, he pressed on, albeit losing a second a lap to the tussling Ferrari and Williams ahead of him. Time after time, Ralf would feint to pass Michael into the final chicane, but each time he would duck back behind, seemingly deciding to wait until their pitstops as Michael was unlikely to make a mistake that would let him past.

Rubens Barrichello passed Jarno Trulli for fourth on the opening lap, but five laps later, when catching Coulthard, he spun coming out of the Casino hairpin, a legacy of having turned off his faltering traction control.

MEMORABLE MOMENT

The first Canadian GP to be held at Montreal's then new circuit, in 1978, might not have been the greatest race, but it yielded the dream result. For victory went to local hero Gilles Villeneuve, and the track was duly named after him. This result had looked unlikely for the Ferrari driver as Jean-Pierre Jarier – replacement for Lotus after Ronnie Peterson's death – dominated from pole. However, Villeneuve worked his way past Jody Scheckter's Wolf to take second. And this became first when the runaway Lotus pulled off with its brakes spent, and Villeneuve reeled off the remaining 20 laps in front of the exultant crowd.

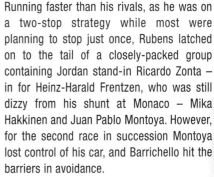

Running faster than his rivals, as he was on a two-stop strategy while most were planning to stop just once, Rubens latched on to the tail of a closely-packed group containing Jordan stand-in Ricardo Zonta – in for Heinz-Harald Frentzen, who was still dizzy from his shunt at Monaco – Mika Hakkinen and Juan Pablo Montoya. However, for the second race in succession Montoya lost control of his car, and Barrichello hit the barriers in avoidance.

Ralf had been carrying more fuel than Michael, and he really flew during the five extra laps in which he stayed out before emerging from his one pit stop in front. The rest of the race was a formality, with Williams, BMW and particularly Michelin better on the day. Hakkinen finally reached the podium, claiming third after passing his slowing team-mate. However, Coulthard was unable to claim the points for fourth as his engine blew, elevating Kimi Räikkönen to equal his record finish, fourth.

Sibling Rivalry: Michael started on pole, but Ra[lf] had swapped places with him by the end, takin[g] the win in the first one-two by a pair of brother[s]

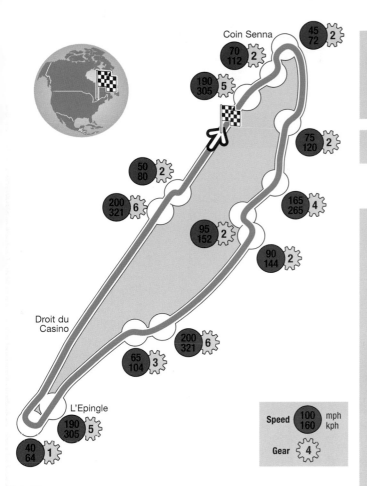

Coin Senna

45 / 72 — gear 2
70 / 112 — gear 2
190 / 305 — gear 5
50 / 80 — gear 2
75 / 120 — gear 2
200 / 321 — gear 6
165 / 265 — gear 4
95 / 152 — gear 2
90 / 144 — gear 2

Droit du Casino

200 / 321 — gear 6
65 / 104 — gear 3
190 / 305 — gear 5
40 / 64 — gear 1

L'Epingle

Speed 100 mph / 160 kph
Gear 4

Pole time
Michael Schumacher, 1m 15.782s, 130.505mph / 209.983kph

Winner's average speed
120.321mph / 193.596kph

Fastest lap
Ralf Schumacher, 1m 17.205s, 128.100mph / 206.113kph

Lap leaders
M Schumacher, 1–45; R Schumacher, 46–69

MONTREAL ROUND 8

Date 10 June 2001 **Laps** 69 **Distance** 189.56 miles / 303.78 km
Weather Warm, dry and bright

RACE RESULTS

Position	Driver	Team	Result	Stops	Qualify Time	Grid
1	Ralf Schumacher	Williams	1h 34m 31.522s	1	1m 16.297s	2
2	Michael Schumacher	Ferrari	1h 34m 51.757s	1	1m 15.782s	1
3	Mika Hakkinen	McLaren	1h 35m 12.194s	1	1m 16.979s	8
4	Kimi Räikkönen	Sauber	1h 35m 39.638s	1	1m 16.875s	7
5	Jean Alesi	Prost	1h 35m 41.957s	1	1m 18.178s	16
6	Pedro de la Rosa	Jaguar	68 laps	2	1m 18.015s	14
7	Ricardo Zonta	Jordan	68 laps	1	1m 17.328s	12
8	Luciano Burti	Prost	68 laps	1	1m 18.753s	19
9	Tarso Marques	Minardi	66 laps	2	1m 20.690s	21
10	Jos Verstappen	Arrows	65 laps	2	1m 17.903s	13
11	Jarno Trulli	Jordan	63 laps (brakes)	1	1m 16.459s	4
R	David Coulthard	McLaren	engine	1	1m 16.423s	3
R	Olivier Panis	BAR	brakes	2	1m 16.771s	6
R	Jacques Villeneuve	BAR	driveshaft	0	1m 17.035s	9
R	Enrique Bernoldi	Arrows	engine	1	1m 18.575s	17
R	Juan Pablo Montoya	Williams	accident	0	1m 17.123s	10
R	Rubens Barrichello	Ferrari	accident	0	1m 16.760s	5
R	Jenson Button	Benetton	oil leak	2	1m 19.033s	20
R	Fernando Alonso	Minardi	driveshaft	0	no time*	22
R	Nick Heidfeld	Sauber	accident	0	1m 17.165s	11
R	Eddie Irvine	Jaguar	accident	0	1m 18.016s	15
R	Giancarlo Fisichella	Benetton	accident	0	1m 18.622s	18

* Qualifying time was disallowed as car's front wing was too low

Getting Serious: Kimi Räikkönen continued to impress, this time with fourth place for Sauber

EUROPEAN GP

NO BROTHERLY LOVE

No doubt upset about being the number two Schumacher at the previous race, Michael turned tough to put Ralf back in his place as Ferrari took control again.

MEMORABLE MOMENT

The 1995 European GP stands out as by far the best race since the modern version of the Nürburgring came into play. This was four races from the end of the championship, but local hero Michael Schumacher was homing in on a second title for Benetton. It was Williams's David Coulthard who led away. But it was drizzling and Jean Alesi's gamble to start with slicks on his Ferrari paid off as the track dried. Coulthard, Damon Hill and Schumacher pitted after three laps, then set about chasing Alesi. However, Schumacher was on a mission and pulled back fully 40 seconds on Alesi, but pitted just as he caught him. Needing to claw back another 24 seconds, Schumacher did just that, muscling his way by Alesi at the chicane with two laps to go.

The Big Squeeze: Michael Schumacher moves across on brother Ralf on the run to the first corner

Michael Schumacher cedes to no one, and he demonstrated that at the start when he was challenged on the run to the first corner by his brother Ralf. Michael simply pulled to his right and kept coming until he was set to put the Williams into the pit wall if Ralf didn't lift. Not wanting to collide, Ralf lifted and Michael held on to the lead. Strong words were exchanged afterwards.

Matters looked good for Michael as he edged away from Ralf in the early laps, but the Michelin tyres were showing how they dropped away before coming good, with Ralf then hauling him back in. Making matters more exciting still, Ralf's team-mate Juan Pablo Montoya was catching both of them.

Running a two-stop strategy, Ralf pitted on the same lap as Michael shortly before mid-distance. After a marginally longer stop, he emerged still behind, with the McLaren of the still-to-pit David Coulthard sandwiched between them on the track. Ralf's challenge wouldn't be allowed to run its natural course, however, as his car was adjudged to have drifted over the white line that separates the pit exit from the track on the run to the first corner as he rejoined the circuit, and he was duly called in for a 10-second stop/go penalty. This dropped Ralf to fourth and elevated Montoya to second.

When Rubens Barrichello made a very late first stop, Ralf was back to third, but Coulthard was running a one-stop race and he moved by into third when Ralf came in for his second planned pit stop.

Never quite able to catch Michael, Montoya was delighted to finish in second place, for only his second finish in nine starts. Coulthard was a further 20 seconds adrift, showing how McLaren had dropped from the forefront. Ralf finished a further eight seconds behind, with Barrichello a dozen seconds adrift. Jarno Trulli looked set to score Jordan's first point in four rounds, but his gearbox failed and so Mika Hakkinen scored for the second race in succession.

A notable pointer to the changing form of the midfield teams was that Jaguar appeared to be matching Jordan as Eddie Irvine pushed Heinz-Harald Frentzen. But neither came away with a point as Irvine ended up stuck on Hakkinen's tail.

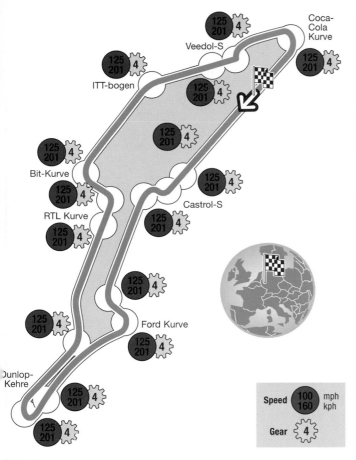

Pole time
Michael Schumacher, 1m 14.950s, 135.979mph / 218.790kph

Winner's average speed
126.854mph / 204.108kph

Fastest lap
Juan Pablo Montoya, 1m 18.354s, 130.075mph / 209.291kph

Lap leaders
M Schumacher, 1–28, 30–67; Montoya, 29

NURBURGRING ROUND 9

Date 24 June 2001 **Laps** 67 **Distance** 189.67 miles / 305.18 km
Weather Warm, dry and bright

RACE RESULTS

Position	Driver	Team	Result	Stops	Qualify Time	Grid
1	Michael Schumacher	Ferrari	1h 29m 42.724s	2	1m 14.950s	1
2	Juan Pablo Montoya	Williams	1h 29m 46.941s	2	1m 15.480s	3
3	David Coulthard	McLaren	1h 30m 07.717s	1	1m 15.717s	5
4	Ralf Schumacher	Williams	1h 30m 16.069s	3	1m 15.228s	2
5	Rubens Barrichello	Ferrari	1h 30m 28.219s	1	1m 15.622s	4
6	Mika Hakkinen	McLaren	1h 30m 47.582s	1	1m 15.776s	6
7	Eddie Irvine	Jaguar	1h 30m 48.922s	1	1m 16.588s	12
8	Pedro de la Rosa	Jaguar	66 laps	1	1m 17.627s	16
9	Jacques Villeneuve	BAR	66 laps	1	1m 16.439s	11
10	Kimi Räikkönen	Sauber	66 laps	1	1m 16.402s	9
11	Giancarlo Fisichella	Benetton	66 laps	2	1m 17.378s	15
12	Luciano Burti	Prost	65 laps	2	1m 18.113s	17
13	Jenson Button	Benetton	65 laps	2	1m 18.626s	20
14	Fernando Alonso	Minardi	65 laps	2	1m 18.630s	21
15	Jean Alesi	Prost	64 laps	1	1m 17.251s	14
R	Jos Verstappen	Arrows	engine	2	1m 18.262s	19
R	Nick Heidfeld	Sauber	driveshaft	1	1m 16.438s	10
R	Heinz-Harald Frentzen	Jordan	traction control	1	1m 16.376s	8
R	Jarno Trulli	Jordan	gearbox	1	1m 16.138s	7
R	Enrique Bernoldi	Arrows	gearbox	1	1m 18.151s	18
R	Olivier Panis	BAR	electronics	0	1m 16.872s	13
R	Tarso Marques	Minardi	electronics	0	1m 18.689s	22

Second Second: Juan Pablo Montoya scored only his second batch of points

FRENCH GP

MICHAEL'S HALF-CENTURY

Not only did Michael Schumacher's sixth win of the year put him 31 points clear of his closest challenger, David Coulthard, but it moved him to within one Grand Prix win of Alain Prost's all-time record of 51.

Making up for the disappointments of events at the Nurburgring, Ralf Schumacher celebrated his twenty-sixth birthday by claiming his first pole position. However, before the race was even underway, everyone was talking about Mika Hakkinen, as the Finn's McLaren had suffered its third grid failure of the year, its gearbox breaking at the start of the parade lap.

As the red lights went out, Ralf led away from Michael with Coulthard narrowly failing to usurp the Ferrari. And this was how they stayed until the first round of pit stops, at which point Ralf lost the lead when his right rear wheel jammed. This lost him

2.5 seconds – a small margin in real life, but not in Formula One, in which every fraction of a second is so significant.

Matters went from bad to worse as Ralf's second set of tyres appeared uncompetitive, and so team-mate Montoya was able to catch him as the race reached mid-distance. Asked to come in and pit or to cede position to his team-mate, Ralf chose the former option, and was followed in a lap later by Michael's Ferrari. Running regally in front, Michael was never troubled thereafter and rattled off his fiftieth grand prix win.

Coulthard had been third after the first round of pit stops, but his race was ruined by speeding at the end of the speed-limit

MEMORABLE MOMENT

Magny-Cours may be bleak when it rains, but it was in such conditions that it enjoyed its greatest race in 1999. Rubens Barrichello led away for Stewart, but McLaren's David Coulthard was fastest in the wet and he soon took the lead. Electrical failure would sideline him, however, and Barrichello took over again. After 44 laps out of 72, Michael Schumacher hit the front for Ferrari, but an early second stop saw Barrichello lead again, with Mika Hakkinen taking over when he pitted. Yet, he too had to pit, and through came Heinz-Harald Frentzen to give Jordan its second win thanks – thanks to having put in extra fuel at Frentzen's one stop early in the race and thus not needing to make another.

zone and having to take a 10-second stop/go penalty. This punishment dropped him to fifth behind Montoya and Rubens Barrichello, who had changed to a three-stop strategy in a bid to climb from his eighth position on the grid. However, Montoya's engine broke soon after his second stop and so the Scot made it to fourth. Although he then caught Barrichello, Coulthard was unable to pass the Brazilian in the remaining 15 laps.

Competitive as always in qualifying, Jarno Trulli finally delivered in the race, finishing in a distant fifth place to give Jordan its first points in five grands prix. The final point was claimed by Nick Heidfeld, who had been lapped in his Sauber, with his team-mate Kimi Räikkönen finishing seventh.

Others who deserved better included Jacques Villeneuve, who parked his BAR early on when its Honda engine cut out, and Eddie Irvine, whose Jaguar lost ground when stuck for many laps behind Heinz-Harald Frentzen's Jordan and then also succumbed to engine failure.

Bravo: Michael Schumacher is greeted, as ever, by Ferrari's delighted mechanics in parc fermé as the *tifosi* go wild worldwide

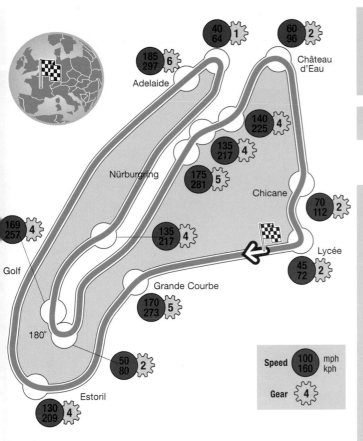

Adelaide
Château d'Eau
Nürburgring
Chicane
Golf
Lycée
Grande Courbe
180°
Estoril

| Speed | 100 160 | mph kph |
| Gear | 4 | |

Pole time
Ralf Schumacher, 1m 12.989s, 130.288mph / 209.633kph

Winner's average speed
121.852mph / 196.06kph

Fastest lap
David Coulthard, 1m 16.088s, 124.982mph / 201.096kph

Lap leaders
R Schumacher, 1–23; M Schumacher, 24–25, 31–45, 51–72;
Coulthard, 26; Montoya, 27–30, 46–50

MAGNY-COURS ROUND 10

Date 1 July 2001 **Laps** 72 **Distance** 190.08 miles / 305.84 km
Weather Hot, dry and bright

RACE RESULTS

Position	Driver	Team	Result	Stops	Qualify Time	Grid
1	Michael Schumacher	Ferrari	1h 33m 35.636s	2	1m 12.999s	2
2	Ralf Schumacher	Williams	1h 33m 46.035s	2	1m 12.989s	1
3	Rubens Barrichello	Ferrari	1h 33m 52.017s	3	1m 13.867s	8
4	David Coulthard	McLaren	1h 33m 52.742s	3	1m 13.186s	3
5	Jarno Trulli	Jordan	1h 34m 43.921s	2	1m 13.310s	5
6	Nick Heidfeld	Sauber	71 laps	2	1m 14.095s	9
7	Kimi Räikkönen	Sauber	71 laps	2	1m 14.536s	13
8	Heinz-Harald Frentzen	Jordan	71 laps	2	1m 13.815s	7
9	Olivier Panis	BAR	71 laps	2	1m 14.181s	11
10	Luciano Burti	Prost	71 laps	2	1m 15.072s	15
11	Giancarlo Fisichella	Benetton	71 laps	2	1m 15.220s	16
12	Jean Alesi	Prost	70 laps	2	1m 15.774s	19
13	Jos Verstappen	Arrows	70 laps	2	1m 15.707s	18
14	Pedro de la Rosa	Jaguar	70 laps	2	1m 15.020s	14
15	Tarso Marques	Minardi	69 laps	2	1m 16.500s	22
16	Jenson Button	Benetton	68 laps	2	1m 15.420s	17
17	Fernando Alonso	Minardi	65 laps	1	1m 16.039s	21
R	Eddie Irvine	Jaguar	engine	2	1m 14.441s	12
R	Juan Pablo Montoya	Williams	engine	2	1m 13.625s	6
R	Enrique Bernoldi	Arrows	engine	0	1m 15.828s	20
R	Jacques Villeneuve	BAR	electronics	0	1m 14.096s	10
R	Mika Hakkinen	McLaren	gearbox	0	1m 13.268s	4

Going nowhere: Mika Hakkinen is stranded on the grid during the parade lap

BRITISH GP

MIKA HITS TOP GEAR

This result was one in the eye for Mika Hakkinen's critics, as the Finn hit the form that made him a double World Champion and trounced everyone. His McLaren team-mate David Coulthard didn't get to see the finish, hurting his title hopes.

MEMORABLE MOMENT

Two cars rubbing wheels at 190mph (306kph) is always going to be memorable. This is what fans were treated to at the 1987 British GP, and this was between team-mates Nelson Piquet and Nigel Mansell. They dominated qualifying for Williams, starting almost one second clear of Ayrton Senna's McLaren. Piquet led from pole and Mansell was forced to pit with a vibration. The new rubber felt good, but Mansell was 28 seconds down with just 29 laps to go. Then the charge started. He got closer and closer but, with four laps to go, his read-out said that he hadn't enough fuel to finish. Yet Mansell kept pressing and caught Piquet on the Hangar Straight with three laps to go. He jinked left and so did Piquet. But a dive down the inside put him through, and he proved his onboard computer wrong as he raced on to win.

Back on Track: Mika Hakkinen was in a class of his own at Silverstone, returning to his winning ways

Mika Hakkinen should have won in Spain, but mechanical failure deprived him. However, his form had been spasmodic since then. But at Silverstone the Finn was back in the groove. This didn't help him to pole, as this went to Michael Schumacher. But it put him back in front of team-mate David Coulthard on the grid for the first time in six races.

Schumacher led away at the start, but he seemed to get it wrong at Copse on lap 5 and the Finn was through. Once in front, he pulled clear, as it became clear that he was running a two-stop strategy and that Ferrari had opted to be more conservative and send Michael out for a one-stop race. Coulthard was already out of the race, though, damaging his title hopes after clashing with Jarno Trulli at the first corner as the Italian was faster away and the Scot didn't want to cede the position. In retrospect, Coulthard needn't have worried, as McLaren had a performance advantage around Silverstone and he would probably have easily passed the Jordan. But, in the heat of the start, Coulthard no doubt thought that he couldn't afford to lose a single position.

This left Juan Pablo Montoya in third after he'd rocketed past Rubens Barrichello, and he soon caught Schumacher's Ferrari, benefiting from being on a two-stop strategy.

Hakkinen was so far clear that he was able to retake the lead shortly after his first stop when Montoya pitted. He was never led again as he found his winning touch for the first time in 2001. Runaway championship leader Schumacher may have been second for six more points, but the 34-second margin of Hakkinen's victory gave him cause for concern that McLaren and the double champion were back on song.

Montoya had more work to do, however, as he re-emerged behind both Ferraris. He was to stay there, too, with Barrichello just coming back on track in front after his one and only stop. At least Montoya made it to the finish for only his third score of the year, unlike team-mate Ralf Schumacher whose engine failed, allowing the Saubers of Kimi Räikkönen and Nick Heidfeld to claim the final points.

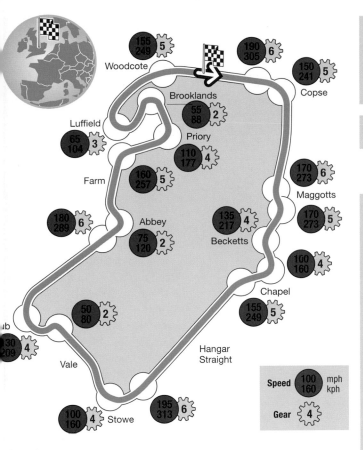

Speed / Gear legend

Woodcote — 155/249 · 5
— 190/305 · 6
Copse — 150/241 · 5
Brooklands — 55/88 · 2
Luffield — 65/104 · 3
Priory — 110/177 · 4
Farm — 160/257 · 5
Maggotts — 170/273 · 6
Abbey — 180/289 · 6 · 75/120 · 2
Becketts — 135/217 · 4 · 170/273 · 5
— 100/160 · 4
Chapel — 155/249 · 5
ub — 30/209 · 4
Vale — 50/80 · 2
Hangar Straight
Stowe — 100/160 · 4 · 195/313 · 6

Speed 100 mph / 160 kph
Gear 4

Pole time
Michael Schumacher, 1m 20.447s, 142.959mph / 230.021kph

Winner's average speed
134.366mph / 216.195kph

Fastest lap
Mika Hakkinen, 1m 23.405s, 137.889mph / 221.863kph

Lap leaders
M Schumacher, 1–4; Hakkinen, 5–21, 25–60; Montoya, 22–24

A Short Race: Jarno Trulli clashed with David Coulthard at the first corner

 SILVERSTONE ROUND 11

Date 15 July 2001 **Laps** 60 **Distance** 191.61 miles / 308.3 km
Weather Warm, dry and bright

RACE RESULTS

Position	Driver	Team	Result	Stops	Qualify Time	Grid
1	Mika Hakkinen	McLaren	1h 25m 33.770s	2	1m 20.529s	2
2	Michael Schumacher	Ferrari	1h 26m 07.416s	1	1m 20.447s	1
3	Rubens Barrichello	Ferrari	1h 26m 33.051s	1	1m 21.715s	6
4	Juan Pablo Montoya	Williams	1h 26m 42.542s	2	1m 22.219s	8
5	Kimi Räikkönen	Sauber	59 laps	2	1m 22.023s	7
6	Nick Heidfeld	Sauber	59 laps	2	1m 22.223s	9
7	Heinz-Harald Frentzen	Jordan	59 laps	2	1m 21.217s	5
8	Jacques Villeneuve	BAR	59 laps	1	1m 22.916s	12
9	Eddie Irvine	Jaguar	59 laps	2	1m 23.439s	15
10	Jos Verstappen	Arrows	58 laps	2	1m 24.067s	17
11	Jean Alesi	Prost	58 laps	1	1m 23.392s	14
12	Pedro de la Rosa	Jaguar	58 laps	2	1m 23.273s	13
13	Giancarlo Fisichella	Benetton	58 laps	2	1m 24.275s	19
14	Enrique Bernoldi	Arrows	58 laps	2	1m 24.606s	20
15	Jenson Button	Benetton	58 laps	2	1m 24.123s	18
16	Fernando Alonso	Minardi	57 laps	2	1m 24.792s	21
R	Ralf Schumacher	Williams	engine	1	1m 22.283s	10
R	Luciano Burti	Prost	engine	0	1m 23.735s	16
R	David Coulthard	McLaren	suspension	0	1m 20.927s	3
R	Jarno Trulli	Jordan	accident	0	1m 20.930s	4
R	Olivier Panis	BAR	accident	0	1m 22.316s	11
NQ*	Tarso Marques	Minardi	-	-	1m 26.506s	22

*Tarso Marques didn't qualify as his best lap was outside the 107% (of pole time) qualifying rule.

GERMAN GP

JUST WILLIAMS

This should have been Juan Pablo Montoya's first Grand Prix win, but the fates decreed otherwise. And there to pick up the pieces was none other than his Williams team-mate Ralf Schumacher for a home win in front of a packed crowd.

The sight of Williams filling the front row was one that everyone expected, given BMW's lead in the horsepower race. Juan Pablo Montoya was more delighted than anyone, as this was his first pole. Mika Hakkinen qualified third, but his McLaren was 0.7 seconds off the pace, with Michael Schumacher's Ferrari a further 0.1 seconds down.

The Williams duo powered away at the start, but it was Michael Schumacher who stood out – unfortunately for the wrong reasons, as he faltered between gears. The pack split around him, then Luciano Burti's Prost shot skywards as it rode over the red car. Both ended up in the gravel trap, with Burti lucky to escape injury. Debris was on the track, but some team managers felt that the race should have continued behind the safety car that had been deployed. However, it was red-flagged and Michael was able to grab his spare car and line up for the restart.

Montoya led away from Ralf again, with Michael tucked in behind, but he was soon dropped. After demoting Hakkinen, the two-stopping Barrichello chased and passed his own team-mate, but there was nothing he could do about the Williams cars, with Montoya well clear. Hakkinen retired early on with engine failure, while seven others retired with engine-related maladies.

Montoya's dreams of victory were shattered when his refuelling rig malfunctioned. The long stop would later cost him a shot at regaining second from Barrichello, as his engine had overheated when stationary and

MEMORABLE MOMENT

Enthusiasts said that Hockenheim would never match the old Nürburgring but, now that it's on the verge of being truncated for 2003, people are starting to reminisce fondly about the circuit with its flat-out blasts through the forests and its ferocious stadium section. The outstanding race here was the 1993 German GP, when Damon Hill looked set for his first win after disappointments in the previous two races. Alain Prost had been delayed by a stop-go penalty and, although he was catching Williams team-mate Hill fast, Hill was 10 seconds clear with a lap-and-a-half to go. But then Hill had a blow-out and Prost came through to win.

failed. Ralf was left to win as he pleased, later claiming that the team-mate for whom he has no affection had brought about his own demise by pressing too hard, a comment that was rubbished by team boss Patrick Head.

Michael moved into second, but as he rejoined after his one planned stop, his car retired with plummeting fuel pressure. Coulthard's hopes of clawing back points came to nought four laps later as he blasted out of the pits and immediately pulled off with engine failure.

So, fully 46 seconds down, Barrichello finished second, with the race's high rate of attrition leaving Jacques Villeneuve to race from twelfth to BAR's second podium placing. Also delighted was Benetton, with Giancarlo Fisichella and Jenson Button finishing fourth and fifth, right on the Canadian's tail. Chasing them hard was Jean Alesi, who claimed sixth for Prost.

How Not to Do It: Burti's Prost flips over Michael Schumacher's stuttering Ferrari

HOCKENHEIM ROUND 12

Date 29 July 2001 **Laps** 45 **Distance** 190.84 miles / 307.06 km
Weather Hot, dry and bright

RACE RESULTS

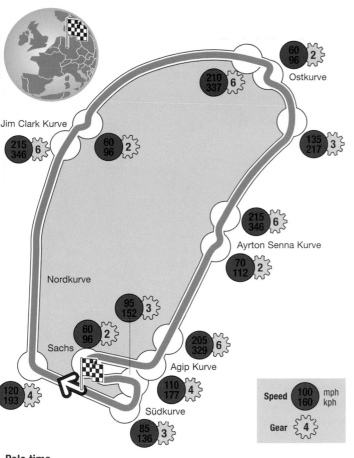

Jim Clark Kurve

215
346 6

Ostkurve

60
96 2

210
337 6

135
217 3

Nordkurve

60
96 2

215
346 6

Ayrton Senna Kurve

95
152 3

70
112 2

Sachs

60
96 2

Agip Kurve

205
329 6

120
193 4

110
177 4

Südkurve

85
136 3

| Speed | 100 / 160 | mph / kph |
| Gear | 4 | |

Position	Driver	Team	Result	Stops	Qualify Time	Grid
1	Ralf Schumacher	Williams	1h 18m 17.873s	1	1m 38.136s	2
2	Rubens Barrichello	Ferrari	1h 19m 03.990s	2	1m 39.682s	6
3	Jacques Villeneuve	BAR	1h 19m 20.679s	1	1m 40.437s	12
4	Giancarlo Fisichella	Benetton	1h 19m 21.350s	1	1m 41.299s	17
5	Jenson Button	Benetton	1h 19m 23.327s	1	1m 41.438s	18
6	Jean Alesi	Prost	1h 19m 23.823s	1	1m 40.724s	14
7	Olivier Panis	BAR	1h 19m 35.400s	2	1m 40.610s	13
8	Enrique Bernoldi	Arrows	44 laps	2	1m 41.668s	19
9	Jos Verstappen	Arrows	44 laps	2	1m 41.870s	20
10	Fernando Alonso	Minardi	44 laps	2	1m 41.913s	21
R	Jarno Trulli	Jordan	hydraulics	1	1m 40.322s	10
R	David Coulthard	McLaren	engine	1	1m 39.574s	5
R	Tarso Marques	Minardi	engine	1	1m 42.716s	22
R	Juan Pablo Montoya	Williams	engine	1	1m 38.117s	1
R	Michael Schumacher	Ferrari	fuel pressure	1	1m 38.941s	4
R	Luciano Burti	Prost	spun off	0	1m 41.213s	16
R	Kimi Räikkönen	Sauber	driveshaft	0	1m 40.072s	8
R	Eddie Irvine	Jaguar	fuel pressure	0	1m 40.371s	11
R	Mika Hakkinen	McLaren	engine	0	1m 38.811s	3
R	Ricardo Zonta	Jordan	crash damage	0	1m 41.174s	15
R	Nick Heidfeld	Sauber	accident	0	1m 39.921s	7
R	Pedro de la Rosa	Jaguar	accident	0	1m 40.265s	9

Pole time
Juan Pablo Montoya, 1m 38.117s, 155.606mph / 250.370kph

Winner's average speed
146.247mph / 235.311kph

Fastest lap
Juan Pablo Montoya, 1m 41.808s, 149.966mph / 241.295kph

Lap leaders
Montoya, 1–22; R Schumacher, 23–45

Williams's Day: Montoya may have faltered, but Williams still won through Ralf Schumacher

HUNGARIAN GP

GAME, SET AND MATCH

Michael Schumacher was in unbeatable form in Hungary, as he not only equalled Alain Prost's record tally of Grand Prix wins but wrapped up his fourth world title, this time with four races to go.

MEMORABLE MOMENT

Arrows has never won a Grand Prix, but the team's wretched record was so nearly brought to a close in 1997. Damon Hill had struggled after leaving Williams at the end of 1996, but the Bridgestone tyres worked well around the endless twists of the Hungaroring, and he tucked in behind Michael Schumacher at the start. Ten laps in, he passed the Ferrari into the first corner as it slithered on blistered tyres. Hill then simply drove away to lead by 30 seconds with three laps to go. But then gearbox problems slowed him and Jacques Villeneuve reeled him in. Hill wasn't giving up, but he was powerless to resist the Williams driver, and was passed with half a lap to go. By way of consolation, Hill was able to hang on to second.

Such was his points advantage as the circus arrived at the Hungaroring that it was always a question of "when" rather than "if" Michael Schumacher would be crowned world champion. McLaren's David Coulthard still stood an outside, mathematical chance, but he would have to win all the remaining races with Ferrari's team leader drawing a blank. And this wasn't likely, especially when Michael qualified on pole by the huge margin of 0.8 seconds. The Scot was second fastest, but this meant that he would start the race on the notoriously dusty side of the track by the pitwall, the side not cleaned by cars on the racing line. Thus it was that Michael blasted clear, followed into the first corner by trusty lieutenant Rubens Barrichello after Coulthard spun his wheels as the five red lights went out and let the Ferrari number two power past. The tight and twisty nature of the circuit meant that he wouldn't easily find a way past to go after Schumacher.

Behind them, Jarno Trulli and Nick Heidfeld touched, without damage, and Eddie Irvine sailed off all on his own, parking his Jaguar in the first corner gravel trap.

So, as Michael eased clear and Coulthard was bottled up behind Barrichello, the order settled for the run to the first round of pit stops. Michael came and went as he pleased, then Barrichello pitted without incident, but Coulthard's crew turned him around just that little bit faster the following lap and he squeezed out in second place. This good work was undone at the second time of asking when Coulthard's fuel nozzle jammed, and so he fell back to third, which is how the leading trio finished.

Schumacher had been untouchable, and was delirious as he completed his slowing-down lap and headed for the podium celebrations. Fourth place belonged to Ralf Schumacher, with Williams not able to make the most of the power advantage that had made the team so dominant at Hockenheim. Team-mate Juan Pablo Montoya struggled home eighth, a lap down. Mika Hakkinen failed to sparkle and ended up fifth, having lost touch with the frontrunners after being bottled up behind Trulli until the Jordan driver was delayed at his first stop. And Nick Heidfeld again put one over his highly-rated team-mate Kimi Räikkönen as the lapped Sauber duo claimed sixth and seventh.

LEFT: Pleased as Punch: Michael Schumacher's traditional jump for joy on the podium had even more momentum behind it as he landed his fourth world title with his 51st grand prix win
OPPOSITE: Job Done: Michael Schumacher punches the sky with delight after wrapping up his fourth Formula One World Championship title, having led throughout save for his pit stops

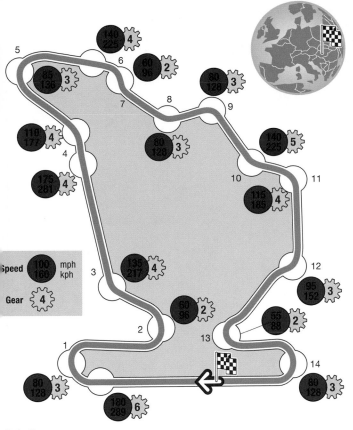

HUNGARORING ROUND 13

Date 19 August 2001 **Laps** 77 **Distance** 190.20 miles / 306.03 km
Weather Very hot, dry and bright

RACE RESULTS

Position	Driver	Team	Result	Stops	Qualify Time	Grid
1	Michael Schumacher	Ferrari	1h 41m 49.675s	2	1m 14.059s	1
2	Rubens Barrichello	Ferrari	1h 41m 53.038s	2	1m 14.953s	3
3	David Coulthard	McLaren	1h 49m 53.615s	2	1m 14.860s	2
4	Ralf Schumacher	Williams	1h 52m 39.362s	2	1m 15.095s	4
5	Mika Hakkinen	McLaren	1h 52m 59.968s	3	1m 15.411s	6
6	Nick Heidfeld	Sauber	76 laps	2	1m 15.739s	7
7	Kimi Räikkönen	Sauber	76 laps	2	1m 15.906s	9
8	Juan Pablo Montoya	Williams	76 laps	2	1m 15.881s	8
9	Jacques Villeneuve	BAR	75 laps	2	1m 16.212s	10
10	Jean Alesi	Jordan	75 laps	2	1m 16.471s	12
11	Pedro de la Rosa	Jaguar	75 laps	2	1m 16.543s	13
12	Jos Verstappen	Arrows	74 laps	2	1m 18.389s	21
R	Giancarlo Fisichella	Benetton	engine	2	1m 16.632s	15
R	Heinz-Harald Frentzen	Prost	spun off	2	1m 17.196s	16
R	Tarso Marques	Minardi	oil pressure	2	1m 19.139s	22
R	Olivier Panis	BAR	hydraulics	3	1m 16.382s	11
R	Jarno Trulli	Jordan	hydraulics	2	1m 15.394s	5
R	Fernando Alonso	Minardi	spun off	1	1m 17.624s	18
R	Jenson Button	Benetton	spun off	2	1m 17.535s	17
R	Enrique Bernoldi	Arrows	spun off	0	1m 18.258s	20
R	Luciano Burti	Prost	spun off	0	1m 18.238s	19
R	Eddie Irvine	Jaguar	accident	0	1m 16.607s	14

Pole time

Michael Schumacher, 1m 14.059s, 120.066mph / 193.186kph

Winner's average speed

112.068mph / 180.317kph

Fastest lap

Mika Hakkinen, 1m 16.723s, 115.900mph / 186.483kph

Lap leaders

M Schumacher, 1–28, 33–52, 55–77; Barrichello, 29–30;
Coulthard, 31–32, 53–54

BELGIAN GP

World Champion Michael Schumacher became the driver with the most Grand Prix wins. But the Ferrari driver's fifty-second victory was made to look easy by his rivals effectively shooting themselves in the foot with a string of mistakes.

Locking Up: Ralf Schumacher leads his brother Michael, but the race was soon to be red-flagged when Luciano Burti crashed

It was no surprise that the Williams drivers occupied the front row, as their BMW engines were always going to dominate up the long climbs. However, Juan Pablo Montoya and Ralf Schumacher's one-two owed just as much to Michelin's dry-weather tyre heating up faster than Bridgestone's. And so it was that they were able to make the jump from intermediates in the closing minutes of a fast-drying qualifying session.

Newly-crowned World Champion Michael Schumacher ended up third, 2.6 seconds down on pole. David Coulthard stayed on intermediates, falling to ninth as others slotted in late laps on dry-weather tyres. Indeed, Prost timed its change to dry tyres to perfection, with Heinz-Harald Frentzen using the Michelins superbly to qualify fourth.

However, Frentzen stalled at the start, leading to the aborting of the start and meaning that he would have to take the restart from the back of the grid. Then Montoya blew his second pole when he stalled at the start of the second formation lap and was also sent to the back. Thus Ralf Schumacher led away, but Michael slipped by into Les Combes. On lap 4, Luciano Burti's Prost touched Eddie Irvine's Jaguar at the 180mph (290kph) Blanchimont corner. The Jaguar spun to a halt, but the Prost slammed into the tyre-wall. The race was stopped while Burti was extricated, unconscious but miraculously in one piece.

At the restart, Williams failed to finish a rear wing beam change to Ralf's car, which was on blocks when the signal came for mechanics to stop working on the cars. So he had to wait for the entire field to pass at the start of the formation lap. Thus Michael led into the first corner, albeit only just from the Benetton of Giancarlo Fisichella which had blasted up from sixth on the grid. Barrichello ran third ahead of Hakkinen and Coulthard as Michael pulled clear.

At the first round of pit stops, Coulthard pitted later than Barrichello but emerged ahead and set about catching Fisichella. He'd spend the next 12 laps discovering how much progress Renault was making with its engine and how good the Michelin tyres were in the cool conditions. After failing to get ahead during their second pit stops, Coulthard moved into second place four laps later, passing Fisichella after both had fumbled their way past Bernoldi's Arrows. The Scot pulled away, but Michael was too far clear and scored the win that made him undisputed leader of the table of all-time wins, surpassing Alain Prost's tally of 51.

Fisichella hung on to third, giving Benetton a huge boost, while Hakkinen was fourth. Jarno Trulli should have finished fifth, but his engine blew, leaving Barrichello to head home a battle in which Trulli's team-mate Jean Alesi just held off Ralf.

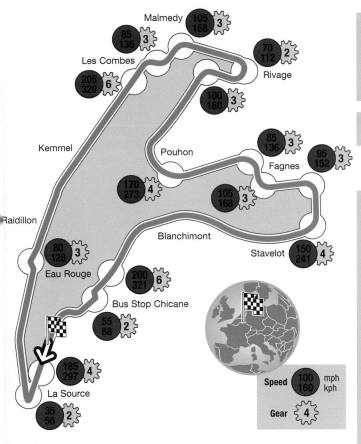

Malmedy
105 / 168 — 3
85 / 138 — 3
70 / 112 — 2
Rivage
100 / 160 — 3
Les Combes
205 / 329 — 6
85 / 136 — 3
95 / 152 — 3
Pouhon
Fagnes
Kemmel
170 / 273 — 4
105 / 168 — 3
Raidillon
Blanchimont
80 / 128 — 3
150 / 241 — 4
Stavelot
Eau Rouge
200 / 321 — 6
Bus Stop Chicane
55 / 88 — 2
185 / 297 — 4
La Source
35 / 56 — 2

Speed 100 mph / 160 kph
Gear 4

Pole time
Juan Pablo Montoya, 1m 52.072s, 139.089mph / 223.794kph

Winner's average speed
137.350mph / 220.996kph

Fastest lap
Michael Schumacher, 1m 49.758s, 142.018mph / 228.507kph

Lap leaders
M Schumacher, 1–36

The race was scheduled for 44 laps but was cut short by one lap when Frentzen stalled on grid, then lost a further seven laps when it had to be stopped so that the circuit could be made safe again following Irvine's and Burti's collision.

 SPA-FRANCORCHAMPS ROUND 14

Date 2 September 2001 **Laps** 36 **Distance** 155.87 miles / 250.795 km
Weather Cool, overcast and dry

RACE RESULTS

Position	Driver	Team	Result	Stops	Qualify Time	Grid
1	Michael Schumacher	Ferrari	1h 08m 05.002s	2	1m 54.685s	3
2	David Coulthard	McLaren	1h 08m 15.100s	2	1m 58.008s	9
3	Giancarlo Fisichella	Benetton	1h 08m 32.744s	2	1m 57.668s	8
4	Mika Hakkinen	McLaren	1h 08m 41.089s	2	1m 57.043s	7
5	Rubens Barrichello	Ferrari	1h 08m 59.523s	2	1m 56.116s	5
6	Jean Alesi	Jordan	1h 09m 04.686s	2	1m 59.128s	13
7	Ralf Schumacher	Williams	1h 09m 04.988s	2	1m 52.959s	2
8	Jacques Villeneuve	BAR	1h 09m 09.972s	2	1m 57.038s	6
9	Heinz-Harald Frentzen	Prost	35 laps	1	1m 55.233s	4
10	Jos Verstappen	Arrows	35 laps	2	2m 02.039s	19
11	Olivier Panis	BAR	35 laps	3	1m 58.838s	11
12	Enrique Bernoldi	Arrows	35 laps	2	2m 03.048s	21
13	Tarso Marques	Minardi	32 laps	4	2m 04.204s	22
R	Jarno Trulli	Jordan	engine	1	1m 59.647s	16
R	Jenson Button	Benetton	accident	0	1m 59.587s	15
R	Juan Pablo Montoya	Williams	engine	0	1m 52.072s	1
R	Pedro de la Rosa	Jaguar	suspension	0	1m 58.519s	10
R	Kimi Räikkönen	Sauber	gearbox	0	1m 59.050s	12
R	Nick Heidfeld	Sauber	suspension	0	1m 59.302s	14
R	Eddie Irvine	Jaguar	accident	0	1m 59.689s	17
R	Luciano Burti	Prost	accident	0	1m 59.900s	18
R	Fernando Alonso	Minardi	gearbox	0	2m 02.594s	20

Miraculous Escape: Luciano Burti's battered Prost shows remarkable rigidity after his shocking, high-speed impact with the tyre-wall at Blanchimont. A car from the early 1990s would probably have collapsed and killed the driver

>> ITALIAN GP

CELEBRATION KEPT IN CHECK

Williams driver Juan Pablo Montoya wanted to explode with delight after scoring his first Grand Prix win, but the terrorist attack on New York earlier in the week kept celebrations to a minimum.

No sooner had the teams arrived at Monza – some having travelled to Italy by train in the interests of security – than stories emerged that many didn't want to race following the destruction of the World Trade Center in New York. The Schumachers were at the vanguard of this groundswell. However, others were anxious that the world must go on and not bow to the terrorists.

As it was, Ferrari removed sponsorship decals from its cars and fitted them with black noses as a mark of respect, while Jaguar blacked out its engine covers and the Jordans carried Stars and Stripes flags. But the Grand Prix went ahead after a minute's silence was observed on Friday and

Sunday. Michael Schumacher wanted to take matters further in the interests of avoiding a first-lap accident like the one in 2000 that killed a marshal. He gathered the drivers together and got them to agree not to overtake into either the first or second chicanes on the opening lap – all of them except Jacques Villeneuve, that is. Then Arrows, Benetton and BAR also requested that their drivers should race without this stipulation. Eventually, Michael Schumacher had to cede when the cars assembled on the grid, as it wasn't clear who would be trying to overtake and who wouldn't.

Mercifully, the start was clean, but Jenson Button hit the back of Jarno Trulli's car at the

first chicane, delaying David Coulthard (who swerved in avoidance) and pushing Mika Hakkinen up the escape road. This allowed the first four on the grid – Juan Pablo Montoya, Rubens Barrichello, Michael Schumacher and also Ralf – to break clear.

Michael passed Ralf early on and the second Williams was dropped, but Montoya wouldn't be swayed. However, he then made a mistake and was passed by Barrichello. It was soon clear that the red cars were running a two-stop strategy, thus explaining their speed on a track that could hardly be more tailor-made for the BMW-powered Williams cars. And so it was that Montoya was back in front when Barrichello – who'd been delayed by a slow first stop – pitted for a second time, and Montoya stayed in the lead as his rear Michelins blistered to win, with the Brazilian being left to rue that recalcitrant fuel rig. Ralf was third, with a subdued Michael fourth. Pedro de la Rosa and Villeneuve brought a little cheer to the beleaguered Jaguar and BMW teams as they claimed the final points.

Not as Planned: Jenson Button caused mayhem at the first corner by hitting Jarno Trulli's Jordan and scattering the field

MEMORABLE MOMENT

No Grand Prix has ever had a more dramatic conclusion than the 1971 Italian race. With no chicanes breaking the flow of the circuit, there had already been 25 changes of lead and there were five cars in a pack fighting for the lead at the start of the final lap. Amazingly, not one of these had won a Grand Prix before. Ronnie Peterson led for March, but François Cevert (Tyrrell), Howden Ganley (BRM) and Mike Hailwood (Surtees) were right with Peter Gethin's BRM at the back of the pack. But the order was shuffled and reshuffled, with Gethin putting two wheels on the grass at the Parabolica but edging ahead to win by 0.01 seconds from Peterson, with all five covered by 0.61 seconds.

100

REVIEW OF 2001

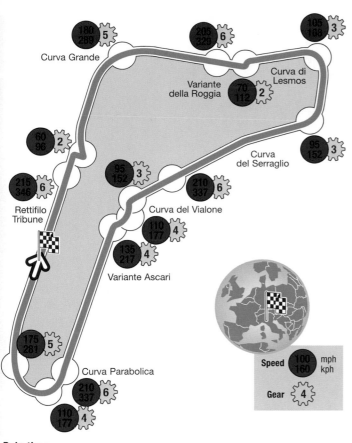

Curva Grande

Variante
della Roggia

Curva di
Lesmos

180
289 | 5

205
329 | 6

105
168 | 3

70
112 | 2

60
96 | 2

95
152 | 3

Curva
del Serraglio

215
346 | 6

95
152 | 3

210
337 | 6

Rettifilo
Tribune

Curva del Vialone

110
177 | 4

135
217 | 4

Variante Ascari

Speed | 100
160 | mph
kph

Gear | 4

175
281 | 5

Curva Parabolica

210
337 | 6

110
177 | 4

Pole time

Juan Pablo Montoya, 1m 22.216s, 150.637mph / 242.375kph

Winner's average speed

148.570mph / 239.049kph

Fastest lap

Ralf Schumacher, 1m 25.073s, 149.412mph / 240.444kph

Lap leaders

Montoya, 1–8, 20–28 and 42–53; Barrichello, 9–19, 36–41;
R Schumacher, 29–35

MONZA ROUND 15

Date 16 September 2001 **Laps** 53 **Distance** 190.61 miles / 306.69 km
Weather Warm, dry and bright

RACE RESULTS

Position	Driver	Team	Result	Stops	Qualify Time	Grid
1	Juan Pablo Montoya	Williams	1h 16m 58.493s	1	1m 22.216s	1
2	Rubens Barrichello	Ferrari	1h 17m 03.668s	2	1m 22.528s	2
3	Ralf Schumacher	Williams	1h 17m 15.828s	1	1m 22.841s	4
4	Michael Schumacher	Ferrari	1h 17m 23.484s	2	1m 22.624s	3
5	Pedro de la Rosa	Jaguar	1h 18m 13.477s	1	1m 23.693s	10
6	Jacques Villeneuve	BAR	1h 18m 20.969s	1	1m 24.164s	15
7	Kimi Räikkönen	Sauber	1h 18m 21.600s	1	1m 23.595s	9
8	Jean Alesi	Jordan	52 laps	2	1m 24.198s	16
9	Olivier Panis	BAR	52 laps	1	1m 24.677s	17
10	Giancarlo Fisichella	Benetton	52 laps	1	1m 24.090s	14
11	Nick Heidfeld	Sauber	52 laps	1	1m 23.417s	8
12	Tomas Enge	Prost	52 laps	1	1m 26.039s	20
13	Fernando Alonso	Minardi	51 laps	2	1m 26.218s	21
R	Enrique Bernoldi	Arrows	engine	1	1m 25.444s	18
R	Alex Yoong	Minardi	spun off	1	1m 27.463s	22
R	Heinz-Harald Frentzen	Prost	gearbox	0	1m 23.943s	12
R	Jos Verstappen	Arrows	engine	0	1m 25.511s	19
R	Mika Hakkinen	McLaren	gearbox	0	1m 23.394s	7
R	Eddie Irvine	Jaguar	engine	0	1m 24.031s	13
R	David Coulthard	McLaren	engine	0	1m 23.148s	6
R	Jenson Button	Benetton	engine	0	1m 23.892s	11
R	Jarno Trulli	Jordan	accident	0	1m 23.126s	5

A Winner at Last: Juan Pablo Montoya controlled matters by running a one-stop strategy to score his first win

UNITED STATES GP

MIKA'S TIMELY REMINDER

Anyone who thought that Mika Hakkinen would glide gently into his 2002 sabbatical only had to watch him channel his anger at Indianapolis to see that he remains one of the sport's greats.

A Parting Shot: Mika Hakkinen channelled his anger to score one more win to take into his sabbatical

Mika Hakkinen was jubilant when he climbed from his McLaren after the United States Grand Prix, but he hadn't been so happy when he'd clambered aboard. The reason for this was that his car had been demoted from second on the grid to fourth as he'd slipped out of the pits when the lights were red in the morning warm-up. A fine would probably have been more fitting, but the anger served the Finn well.

Michael Schumacher led away from pole position, with Juan Pablo Montoya's Williams offering a challenge on the run to the first corner. Thereafter, Schumacher was pushed by a flying Rubens Barrichello. Indeed, such

was the Brazilian's pace that he closed and passed for the lead, making it clear that he was running a two-stop race. The Ferraris were followed by both Williams drivers then the two McLarens. And this was how it stayed until Barrichello pitted at one third distance. He rejoined in fifth as the others kept on going, a clear indication that they all planned to stop just the once.

Montoya then caught Schumacher and delighted his many fans by taking the lead mid-race. However, his engine failed just after he rejoined and so Ferrari regained the advantage. By stopping very late, though, Hakkinen slipped into the lead, chased hard by Barrichello. Likewise, Schumacher was chased by Coulthard as his brother Ralf had spun off two laps before Montoya stopped,

MEMORABLE MOMENT

Indianapolis has hosted a Grand Prix only twice, but it is for its Indy 500 that it's most famous. And the most exciting of these was the 1963 event, when it looked as though the British-built rear-engined cars were going to overturn the old-fashioned American roadsters for the first time. Parnelli Jones led into the closing laps, but his car was leaking oil as Jim Clark closed in for Lotus. Leaking oil traditionally spells a black flag at Indianapolis, but national pride was at stake and the flag was never waved. Moreover, by the time this could be checked properly, the oil had dropped below the level of the leak and so Jones' car was allowed to continue. Thus, Jones won and Clark ended up second, but he was to strike back with victory in 1965.

following a good battle with Sauber's Nick Heidfeld.

With just four laps to go, Barrichello's engine began to sound weak and, two slowing laps later, it failed, elevating Michael to second and David Coulthard to third, helping no end the Scot's bid to end the year as runner-up.

Jarno Trulli finished fourth, 45.5 seconds down on Coulthard, but Jordan was denied valuable points when his undercar plank failed to pass scrutineering. This promoted Eddie Irvine, Heidfeld (who was right on his tail) and Jean Alesi. However, Trulli's disqualification was later overturned on a technicality and he got to keep fourth.

Hakkinen said afterwards that he'd always wanted to add a British GP win to his tally, and to add the US GP as well was extra special. Everyone present was delighted that his troubled season had produced another win to take with him into his sabbatical.

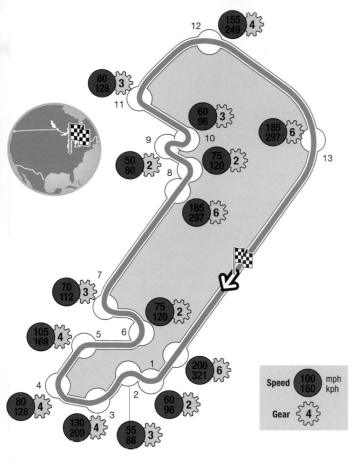

Date 30 September 2001 **Laps** 73 **Distance** 190.16 miles / 305.97 km
Weather Warm, dry and bright

RACE RESULTS

Position	Driver	Team	Result	Stops	Qualify Time	Grid
1	Mika Hakkinen	McLaren	1h 32m 42.840s	1	1m 12.309s	4*
2	Michael Schumacher	Ferrari	1h 32m 53.886s	1	1m 11.708s	1
3	David Coulthard	McLaren	1h 32m 54.883s	1	1m 12.500s	7
4	Jarno Trulli	Jordan	1h 33m 40.263s	1	1m 12.605s	8
5	Eddie Irvine	Jaguar	1h 33m 55.274s	1	1m 13.189s	14
6	Nick Heidfeld	Sauber	1h 33m 55.836s	2	1m 12.434s	6
7	Jean Alesi	Jordan	72 laps	1	1m 12.607s	9
8	Giancarlo Fisichella	Benetton	72 laps	1	1m 12.942s	12
9	Jenson Button	Benetton	72 laps	1	1m 12.805s	10
10	Heinz-Harald Frentzen	Prost	72 laps	1	1m 13.281s	15
11	Olivier Panis	BAR	72 laps	1	1m 13.122s	13
12	Pedro de la Rosa	Jaguar	72 laps	1	1m 13.679s	16
13	Enrique Bernoldi	Arrows	72 laps	1	1m 14.129s	19
14	Tomas Enge	Prost	72 laps	1	1m 14.185s	21
15	Rubens Barrichello	Ferrari	engine	2	1m 12.327s	5
R	Jacques Villeneuve	BAR	crash damage	1	1m 14.012s	18
R	Jos Verstappen	Arrows	engine	1	1m 14.138s	20
R	Juan Pablo Montoya	Williams	engine	1	1m 12.252s	3
R	Alex Yoong	Minardi	gearbox	1	1m 15.247s	22
R	Ralf Schumacher	Williams	spun off	1	1m 11.986s	2
R	Fernando Alonso	Minardi	driveshaft	1	1m 13.991s	17
R	Kimi Räikkönen	Sauber	driveshaft	1	1m 12.881s	11

Trulli was disqualified for an irregularity on his car's skid block, but was later reinstated.
* Hakkinen qualified second fastest in 1m 11.945s, but his best lap was disallowed
as he passed a red light at the pit exit in the warm-up.

Pole time
Michael Schumacher, 1m 11.708s, 130.775mph / 210.417kph

Winner's average speed
123.061mph / 198.005kph

Fastest lap
Juan Pablo Montoya, 1m 14.448s, 125.962mph / 202.673kph

Lap leaders
M Schumacher, 1–4, 27–33, 36–38; Barrichello, 5–26, 46–49;
Montoya, 34–35; Hakkinen, 39–45, 50–73

Patriot Games: Everyone stands for the American national anthem

JAPANESE GP

OVER AND OUT

Michael Schumacher rounded out the year in the style of a champion in a race that marked the end of the careers of both Jean Alesi and Mika Hakkinen.

Michael Schumacher had appeared out of sorts both at Monza and Indianapolis, but he was back in form at Suzuka. At this drivers' circuit, he secured pole by fully 0.7 seconds. The fact that he did this in a car that was carrying development parts for this year's car didn't escape the notice of his rivals, who were left reeling by his pace through the tricky esses.

Schumacher's principal aim, though, was to help his Ferrari team-mate Rubens Barrichello to overhaul McLaren's David Coulthard in order to take second in the drivers' rankings. However, the Scot held a seven-point advantage, so this required a win for the Brazilian, with Coulthard coming no higher than fifth.

As Barrichello was separated from Schumacher by the Williams duo, Ferrari decided that he would have to start very light on fuel and try to get up into second at the start. Then, Michael would move over and let him escape, holding up those behind so that Rubens could call in not twice, but three times, for fuel. Ralf Schumacher was despatched on the opening lap, but Barrichello was forced to take to the grass as he passed Juan Pablo Montoya into the chicane on lap two. It was a hairy move and he only made it past as the Colombian made space, but Montoya then retook him and was never caught again.

Barrichello's day went from bad to worse when his engine stalled briefly during his second pit stop. However, by then, his hopes had been dashed and so the 2001 runner-up spot was taken by Coulthard, who was elevated to third, some distance behind Montoya by the chequered flag, when team-mate Mika Hakkinen let him through for the final podium position.

Hakkinen had looked carefree all weekend. He talked still of this being his last race before a one-year sabbatical, but most believe that it was the last before his retirement for good. Either way, the Finn was noticeably relaxed, and fourth place just ahead of Barrichello and Ralf Schumacher showed that he hadn't backed off that much.

The other driver bowing out, Jean Alesi, had a more dramatic departure, being caught out when Kimi Räikkönen spun in front of him at Dunlop Curve, putting both of them into the barriers. Both escaped injury.

LEFT: Over and Out: A spinning Kimi Räikkönen left Jean Alesi nowhere to go, taking him out of his final grand prix earlier than planned. Fortunately, both were uninjured in this hefty accident
OPPOSITE: Number Nine: Michael Schumacher was pushed hard by Juan Pablo Montoya, but won as he pleased to round out his championship year with his ninth win, this his 53rd in all

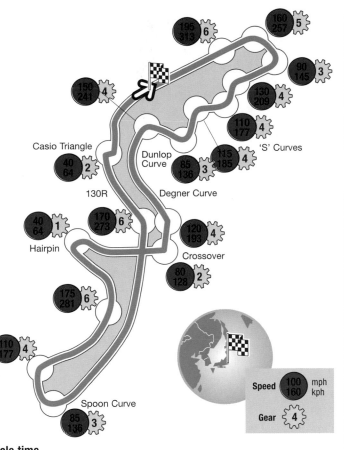

Pole time
Michael Schumacher, 1m 32.484s, 141.845mph / 228.229kph

Winner's average speed
132.145mph / 212.621kph

Fastest lap
Ralf Schumacher, 1m 36.944s, 135.319mph / 217.728kph

Lap leaders
M Schumacher, 1–18, 24–36, 39–53; R Schumacher, 22–23;
Montoya, 19–21, 37–38

SUZUKA ROUND 17

Date 14 October 2001 **Laps** 53 **Distance** 193.00 miles / 310.5 km
Weather Warm, dry and bright

RACE RESULTS

Position	Driver	Team	Result	Stops	Qualify Time	Grid
1	Michael Schumacher	Ferrari	1h 27m 33.298s	2	1m 32.484s	1
2	Juan Pablo Montoya	Williams	1h 27m 36.452s	2	1m 33.184s	2
3	David Coulthard	McLaren	1h 27m 56.560s	2	1m 33.916s	7
4	Mika Hakkinen	McLaren	1h 28m 08.837s	2	1m 33.662s	5
5	Rubens Barrichello	Ferrari	1h 28m 09.842s	3	1m 33.323s	4
6	Ralf Schumacher	Williams	1h 28m 10.420s	3	1m 33.297s	3
7	Jenson Button	Benetton	1h 29m 10.400s	2	1m 34.375s	9
8	Jarno Trulli	Jordan	52 laps	2	1m 34.002s	8
9	Nick Heidfeld	Sauber	52 laps	2	1m 34.375s	10
10	Jacques Villeneuve	BAR	52 laps	2	1m 35.109s	14
11	Fernando Alonso	Minardi	52 laps	2	1m 36.410s	18
12	Heinz-Harald Frentzen	Prost	52 laps	3	1m 35.132s	15
13	Olivier Panis	BAR	51 laps	2	1m 35.766s	17
14	Enrique Bernoldi	Arrows	51 laps	3	1m 36.885s	20
15	Jos Verstappen	Arrows	51 laps	3	1m 36.973s	21
16	Alex Yoong	Minardi	50 laps	2	1m 38.246s	22
17	Giancarlo Fisichella	Benetton	gearbox	2	1m 33.830s	6
R	Pedro de la Rosa	Jaguar	oil leak	2	1m 35.639s	16
R	Tomas Enge	Prost	brakes	4	1m 36.446s	19
R	Eddie Irvine	Jaguar	refuelling rig	1	1m 34.851s	13
R	Kimi Räikkönen	Sauber	accident	-	1m 34.581s	12
R	Jean Alesi	Jordan	accident	-	1m 34.420s	11

Note

Drivers are listed according to their finishing position in each race

Scoring System

First, **10 points**; second, **6 points**; third, **4 points**; fourth, **3 points**; fifth, **2 points**; sixth, **1 point**

Driver	Nationality	Car-Engine	1 March 4, Australian GP	2 March 18, Malaysian GP	3 April 1, Brazilian GP	4 April 15, San Marino GP
Michael Schumacher	GER	Ferrari F2001	1PF	1P	2P	R
David Coulthard	GBR	McLaren-Mercedes MP4-16	2	3	1	2P
Rubens Barrichello	BRA	Ferrari F2001	3	2	R	3
Ralf Schumacher	GER	Williams-BMW FW23	R	5	RF	1F
Mika Hakkinen	FIN	McLaren-Mercedes MP4-16	R	6F	R	4
Juan Pablo Montoya	COL	Williams-BMW FW23	R	R	R	7
Nick Heidfeld	GER	Sauber-Petronas C20	4	R	3	R
Jarno Trulli	ITA	Jordan-Honda EJ11	R	8	5	5
Jacques Villeneuve	CAN	BAR-Honda 003	R	R	7	R
Kimi Räikkönen	FIN	Sauber-Petronas C20	6	R	R	R
Giancarlo Fisichella	ITA	Benetton-Renault B201	13	R	6	R
Heinz-Harald Frentzen	GER	Jordan-Honda EJ11	5	4	11	6
Heinz-Harald Frentzen	GER	Prost-Acer AP04	-	-	-	-
Eddie Irvine	GBR	Jaguar R2	11	R	R	R
Jean Alesi	FRA	Prost-Acer AP04	9	9	8	9
Jean Alesi	FRA	Jordan-Honda EJ11	-	-	-	-
Olivier Panis	FRA	BAR-Honda 003	7	R	4	8
Pedro de la Rosa	SPA	Jaguar R2	-	-	-	-
Jenson Button	GBR	Benetton-Renault B201	14	11	10	12
Jos Verstappen	HOL	Arrows-Asiatech A22	10	7	R	R
Fernando Alonso	SPA	Minardi-European PS01	12	13	R	R
Enrique Bernoldi	BRA	Arrows-Asiatech A22	R	R	R	10
Luciano Burti	BRA	Jaguar R2	8	10	R	11
Luciano Burti	BRA	Prost-Acer AP04	-	-	-	-
Tomas Enge	CZE	Prost-Acer AP04	-	-	-	-
Tarso Marques	BRA	Minardi-European PS01	R	14	9	R
Gaston Mazzacane	ARG	Prost-Acer AP04	R	12	R	R
Alex Yoong	MAL	Minardi-European PS01	-	-	-	-
Ricardo Zonta	BRA	Jordan-Honda EJ11	-	-	-	-

	Constuctor	1 March 4, Australian GP	2 March 18, Malaysian GP	3 April 1, Brazilian GP	4 April 15, San Marino GP
1	Ferrari	14	16	6	4
2	McLaren-Mercedes	6	5	10	9
3	Williams-BMW	-	2	-	10
4	Sauber-Petronas	4	-	4	-
5	Jordan-Honda	2	3	2	3
6	BAR-Honda	-	-	3	-
7	Benetton-Renault	-	-	1	-
8	Jaguar	-	-	-	-
9	Prost-Acer	-	-	-	-
10	Arrows-Asiatech	-	-	-	-
	Minardi-European	-	-	-	-

Symbols

D disqualified
F fastest lap
NS non-starter
P pole position
R retired

2001 Final Tables

Drivers (continued, rounds 7–17)

7 May 27, Monaco GP	8 June 10, Canadian GP	9 June 24, European GP	10 July 1, French GP	11 July 15, British GP	12 July 29, German GP	13 August 19, Hungarian GP	14 September 2, Belgian GP	15 September 16, Italian GP	16 September 30, United States GP	17 October 14, Japanese GP	Points Total
1	2P	1P	1	2P	R	1P	1F	4	2P	1P	123
5PF	R	3	4F	R	R	3	2	R	3	3	65
2	R	5	3	3	2	2	5	2	15	5	56
R	1F	4	2P	R	1	4	7	3F	R	6F	49
R	3	6	R	1F	R	5F	4	R	1	4	37
R	R	2F	R	4	RPF	8	RP	1P	RF	2	31
R	R	R	6	6	R	6	R	11	6	9	12
4	11	R	5	8	3	9	8	R	4	8	12
10	R	9	R	5	R	7	R	6	R	10	12
R	4	10	7	13	4	R	3	7	R	R	9
R	R	11	11	7	-	-	9	10	8	17	8
-	NS	R	8	-	-	R	-	-	-	-	6
3	-	-	-	9	R	R	R	R	10	12	6
6	R	7	R	11	6	-	-	-	5	R	5
-	5	15	12	-	-	10	6	8	7	R	5
R	-	-	-	R	7	R	11	9	11	13	3
R	R	R	9	12	R	11	R	5	12	R	2
7	6	8	14	15	5	R	R	R	9	7	1
8	R	13	16	10	9	12	10	R	R	15	
R	10	R	13	16	10	R	R	13	R	11	
9	R	14	17	14	8	R	12	R	13	14	
R	R	R	R	R	R	R	R	-	-	R	
-	-	-	-	NS	-	-	-	-	14	16	
R	8	12	10	-	R	R	13	12	-	-	
R	9	R	15	-	R	-	-	R	R	-	
-	7	-	-	-	R	-	-	-	-	-	

Constructors (continued, rounds 7–17)

7 May 27, Monaco GP	8 June 10, Canadian GP	9 June 24, European GP	10 July 1, French GP	11 July 15, British GP	12 July 29, German GP	13 August 19, Hungarian GP	14 September 2, Belgian GP	15 September 16, Italian GP	16 September 30, United States GP	17 October 14, Japanese GP	Points Total
16	6	12	14	10	6	16	12	9	6	12	179
2	4	5	3	10	-	6	9	-	14	7	102
-	10	9	6	3	10	3	-	14	-	7	80
-	3	-	1	3	-	1	-	-	1	-	21
-	-	-	2	-	-	-	1	1	3	-	19
3	-	-	-	-	4	-	4	-	-	-	17
-	-	-	-	-	5	-	-	1	-	-	10
4	1	-	-	-	-	-	-	2	2	-	9
1	2	-	-	-	1	-	-	-	-	-	4
-	-	-	-	-	-	-	-	-	-	-	1
-	-	-	-	-	-	-	-	-	-	-	

2001
FINAL TABLES

GLAMOUR ON THE GRID

A World of Red: Promotional girls are employed by sponsors to add welcome glamour to the grid. And yes, those are wigs...

I Love Ferrari: The world's most popular team by a country mile is Ferrari. These *tifosi* are at their spiritual home, Monza, for the Italian GP

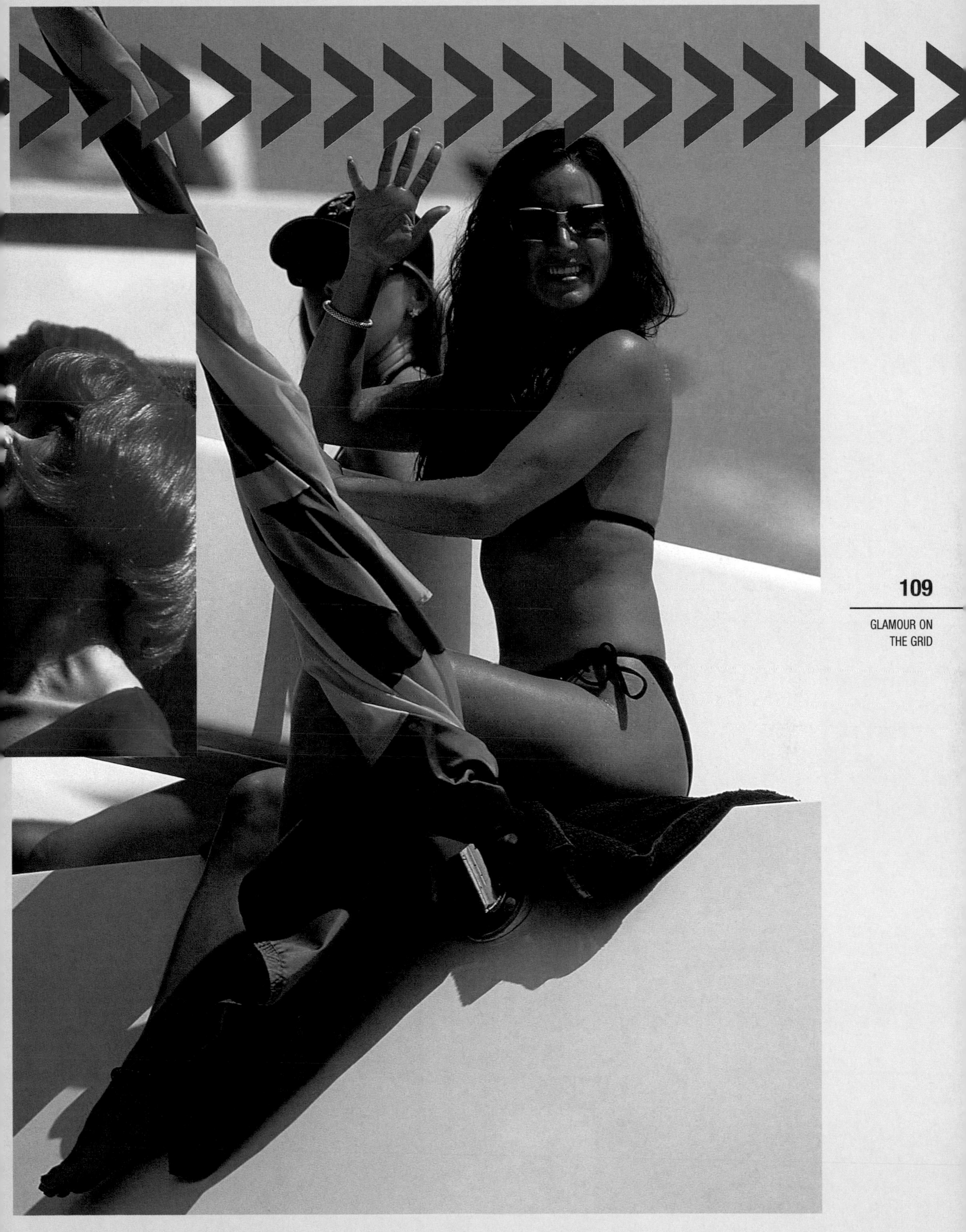

Famous Partners: Formula One is renowned for its drivers having extremely glamorous girlfriends. This is Brazilian model Simone Abdelnour, David Coulthard's partner through 2001

On the Ball: Legendary footballer Pele regales fellow Brazilian Luciano Burti with an amusing anecdote at the Brazilian GP at Interlagos

Busy on the Grid: The grid is always packed with the rich and famous in the countdown to the start. But some are there working, such as the author, seen interviewing Ferrari's Ross Brawn at the bottom right of the photo

F1 RECORDS

GRAND PRIX CHRONOLOGY

1950 First FIA World Championship for cars with 1.5-litre supercharged or 4.5-litre normally-aspirated engines. Indy 500 is included as a round, but no F1 teams attend.

1951 BRM and Girling introduce disc brakes.

1952 Championship is run for cars with 2-litre normally-aspirated engines, that's to say F2 cars.

1954 Maximum engine capacity increased to 2.5 litres. Supercharged engines are re-admitted if less than 750cc. Minimum race duration of 500km or three hours.

1958 Minimum race duration of 300km or two hours imposed. Stirling Moss scores first rear-engined win.

The First: Giuseppe Farina after winning the first World Championship Grand Prix

1960 Final win for a rear-engined car. Last year for Indy 500 in championship.

1961 Maximum engine capacity is 1.5-litre normally-aspirated, with a weight limit of 450kg. Commercial fuel becomes mandatory in place of Avgas. Supercharged engines are banned.

1962 Monocoque Lotus revolutionises F1.

1966 Debut season for 3-litre formula with a 500kg weight limit.

1967 Ford Cosworth DFV, the most successful F1 engine ever, wins on debut. Aerodynamic wings seen for first time above engine.

1968 Wings put on supports to become spoilers, both above front and rear axles. Gold Leaf Lotus heralds age of sponsorship.

1969 Onboard extinguishers and roll-hoops made mandatory. Four-wheel drive is toyed with. Moveable aerodynamic devices are banned mid-year.

1970 Bag fuel tanks made mandatory. Minimum weight is 530kg.

1971 Slick tyres are introduced. Lotus tries a gas turbine engine.

1972 Engines with more than 12 cylinders are banned.

1973 Maximum fuel tank size is 250 litres, minimum weight is 575kg. Breathable air driver safety system introduced.

1974 Rear wing overhang limited to 1m behind rear axle.

1975 Hesketh and Hill try carbonfibre aerodynamic parts.

1976 Rear wing overhang cut back to 80cm. Tall air boxes banned from Spanish GP. McLaren introduces Kevlar and Nomex in its structure.

1977 Renault's RS01 brings 1.5-litre turbo engines to F1. Lotus introduces ground effect.

1978 Brabham's 'fan car' wins Swedish GP and is banned. Tyrrell tests active suspension.

1979 Renault's Jean-Pierre Jabouille scores first turbo win.

1980 Brabham introduces carbon brake discs.

1981 McLaren's carbonfibre monocoque revolutionises F1 car construction. Sliding skirts are banned and 6cm ground clearance enforced. Minimum weight now 585kg.

1982 Survival cells made mandatory. Brabham introduces refuelling pit stops.

1983 Brabham's Nelson Piquet and BMW become first turbo world champions. Ground effect is banned and flat bottoms introduced. Michele Alboreto scores last DFV win. Minimum weight cut to 540kg.

1984 Fuel tank cut to 220 litres. Mid-race refuelling banned.

1985 Crash-tested nose box becomes mandatory.

1986 Normally-aspirated engines are banned as F1 goes all-turbo, with maximum fuel capacity of 195 litres.

1987 3.5-litre normally-aspirated engines introduced alongside turbos, with 500kg minimum weight limit against turbos' 540kg. Turbos limited to 4 bar boost.

1988 Pop-off boost limited to 2.5 bar and fuel allowance for turbo cars cut to 150 litres. Drivers' feet must be behind front axle.

1989 Turbo engines banned and fuel tank capacity cut to 150 litres for normally-aspirated engines. Ferrari introduces semi-automatic gearboxes.

1992 Top teams use driver aids such as active suspension, traction control and anti-lock brakes.

1994 Driver aids outlawed. Refuelling pit stops permitted again. Ayrton Senna and Roland Ratzenberger die at Imola, triggering rule changes and introducing more chicanes to slow cars at fast circuits.

1995 Engine capacity cut to 3.0 litres. Wing size reduced to cut downforce.

1996 Higher cockpit-side protection made mandatory. Aerodynamic suspension parts banned.

1998 Chassis made narrower. Grooved tyres introduced and slicks banned in order to slow the cars.

1999 Extra groove is added to front and rear tyres.

2001 Traction control is permitted from Spanish GP onwards.

WORLD CHAMPIONS

DRIVERS

1950	Giuseppe Farina	Alfa Romeo
1951	Juan Manuel Fangio	Alfa Romeo
1952	Alberto Ascari	Ferrari
1953	Alberto Ascari	Ferrari
1954	Juan Manuel Fangio	
		Maserati & Mercedes
1955	Juan Manuel Fangio	Mercedes
1956	Juan Manuel Fangio	Ferrari
1957	Juan Manuel Fangio	Maserati
1958	Mike Hawthorn	Ferrari
1959	Jack Brabham	Cooper
1960	Jack Brabham	Cooper
1961	Phil Hill	Ferrari
1962	Graham Hill	BRM
1963	Jim Clark	Lotus
1964	John Surtees	Ferrari
1965	Jim Clark	Lotus
1966	Jack Brabham	Brabham
1967	Denny Hulme	Brabham
1968	Graham Hill	Lotus
1969	Jackie Stewart	Matra
1970	Jochen Rindt	Lotus
1971	Jackie Stewart	Tyrrell
1972	Emerson Fittipaldi	Lotus
1973	Jackie Stewart	Tyrrell
1974	Emerson Fittipaldi	McLaren
1975	Niki Lauda	Ferrari
1976	James Hunt	McLaren
1977	Niki Lauda	Ferrari
1978	Mario Andretti	Lotus
1979	Jody Scheckter	Ferrari
1980	Alan Jones	Williams
1981	Nelson Piquet	Brabham
1982	Keke Rosberg	Williams
1983	Nelson Piquet	Brabham
1984	Niki Lauda	McLaren
1985	Alain Prost	McLaren
1986	Alain Prost	McLaren
1987	Nelson Piquet	Williams
1988	Ayrton Senna	McLaren
1989	Alain Prost	McLaren
1990	Ayrton Senna	McLaren
1991	Ayrton Senna	McLaren
1992	Nigel Mansell	Williams
1993	Alain Prost	Williams
1994	Michael Schumacher	Benetton
1995	Michael Schumacher	Benetton
1996	Damon Hill	Williams
1997	Jacques Villeneuve	Williams
1998	Mika Hakkinen	McLaren
1999	Mika Hakkinen	McLaren
2000	Michael Schumacher	Ferrari
2001	Michael Schumacher	Ferrari

CONSTRUCTORS

1958	Vanwall
1959	Cooper-Climax
1960	Cooper-Climax
1961	Ferrari
1962	BRM
1963	Lotus-Climax
1964	Ferrari
1965	Lotus-Climax
1966	Brabham-Repco
1967	Brabham-Repco
1968	Lotus-Ford DFV
1969	Matra-Ford DFV
1970	Lotus-Ford DFV
1971	Tyrrell-Ford DFV
1972	Lotus-Ford DFV
1973	Lotus-Ford DFV
1974	McLaren-Ford DFV
1975	Ferrari
1976	Ferrari
1977	Ferrari
1978	Lotus-Ford DFV
1979	Ferrari
1980	Williams-Ford DFV
1981	Williams-Ford DFV
1982	Ferrari
1983	Ferrari
1984	McLaren-TAG
1985	McLaren-TAG
1986	Williams-Honda
1987	Williams-Honda
1988	McLaren-Honda
1989	McLaren-Honda
1990	McLaren-Honda
1991	McLaren-Honda
1992	Williams-Renault
1993	Williams-Renault
1994	Williams-Renault
1995	Benetton-Renault
1996	Williams-Renault
1997	Williams-Renault
1998	McLaren-Mercedes
1999	Ferrari
2000	Ferrari
2001	Ferrari

McLaren Ace: Ayrton Senna, showed on his McLaren debut in 1988, won all of his three world titles with the McLaren team

The Greatest Ever?: Fangio – five-time World Champion – stunned onlookers with his drive from behind to win the German GP in 1957

MOST GRANDS PRIX STARTS

DRIVERS

256	Riccardo Patrese	ITA		Derek Warwick	GBR
210	Gerhard Berger	AUT	146	Carlos Reutemann	ARG
208	Andrea de Cesaris	ITA	144	Emerson Fittipaldi	BRA
204	Nelson Piquet	BRA	135	Jean-Pierre Jarier	FRA
201	Jean Alesi	FRA	132	Eddie Cheever	USA
199	Alain Prost	FRA		Clay Regazzoni	SUI
194	Michele Alboreto	ITA	130	Eddie Irvine	GBR
187	Nigel Mansell	GBR	129	Heinz-Harald Frentzen	GER
176	Graham Hill	GBR	128	Mario Andretti	USA
175	Jacques Laffite	FRA	126	Jack Brabham	AUS
171	Niki Lauda	AUT	124	David Coulthard	GBR
163	Thierry Boutsen	BEL	123	Ronnie Peterson	SWE
162	Mika Hakkinen	FIN	119	Pierluigi Martini	ITA
	Johnny Herbert	GBR	116	Jacky Ickx	BEL
	Michael Schumacher	GER		Damon Hill	GBR
161	Ayrton Senna	BRA		Alan Jones	AUS
158	Martin Brundle	GBR	114	Keke Rosberg	FIN
152	John Watson	GBR		Patrick Tambay	FRA
149	René Arnoux	FRA	112	Denny Hulme	NZL
147	Rubens Barrichello	BRA		Jody Scheckter	RSA

CONSTRUCTORS

653	Ferrari	409	Prost	230	March
526	McLaren	394	Brabham	197	BRM
490	Lotus	371	Arrows	180	Jordan
445	Williams	317	Benetton	132	Osella
418	Tyrrell	271	Minardi	129	Cooper

MOST WINS

DRIVERS

53	Michael Schumacher	GER		Alan Jones	AUS
51	Alain Prost	FRA		Carlos Reutemann	ARG
41	Ayrton Senna	BRA	11	David Coulthard	GBR
31	Nigel Mansell	GBR		Jacques Villeneuve	CDN
27	Jackie Stewart	GBR	10	Gerhard Berger	AUT
25	Jim Clark	GBR		James Hunt	GBR
	Niki Lauda	AUT		Ronnie Peterson	SWE
24	Juan Manuel Fangio	ARG		Jody Scheckter	RSA
23	Nelson Piquet	BRA	8	Denny Hulme	NZL
22	Damon Hill	GBR		Jacky Ickx	BEL
20	Mika Hakkinen	FIN	7	René Arnoux	FRA
16	Stirling Moss	GBR	6	Tony Brooks	GBR
14	Jack Brabham	AUS		Jacques Laffite	FRA
	Emerson Fittipaldi	BRA		Riccardo Patrese	FRA
	Graham Hill	GBR		Jochen Rindt	AUT
13	Alberto Ascari	ITA		John Surtees	GBR
12	Mario Andretti	USA		Gilles Villeneuve	CDN

CONSTRUCTORS

144	Ferrari	15	Renault		Wolf
134	McLaren	10	Alfa Romeo	2	Honda
106	Williams	9	Ligier	1	Eagle
79	Lotus		Maserati		Hesketh
35	Brabham		Matra		Penske
27	Benetton		Mercedes		Porsche
23	Tyrrell		Vanwall		Shadow
17	BRM	3	Jordan		Stewart
16	Cooper		March		

MOST WINS IN ONE SEASON

DRIVERS

9	Nigel Mansell	GBR	1992		Ayrton Senna	BRA	1991
	M Schumacher	GER	1995		J Villeneuve	CDN	1997
	M Schumacher	GER	2000	**6**	Mario Andretti	USA	1978
	M Schumacher	GER	2001		Alberto Ascari	ITA	1952
8	Mika Hakkinen	FIN	1998		Jim Clark	GBR	1965
	Damon Hill	GBR	1996		Juan M Fangio	ARG	1954
	M Schumacher	GER	1994		Damon Hill	GBR	1994
	Ayrton Senna	BRA	1988		James Hunt	GBR	1976
7	Jim Clark	GBR	1963		Nigel Mansell	GBR	1987
	Alain Prost	FRA	1984		M Schumacher	GER	1998
	Alain Prost	FRA	1988		Ayrton Senna	BRA	1989
	Alain Prost	FRA	1993		Ayrton Senna	BRA	1990

CONSTRUCTORS

15	McLaren	1988		Williams	1997		Ferrari	1979
12	McLaren	1984	**7**	Ferrari	1952		Ferrari	1990
	Williams	1996		Ferrari	1953		Ferrari	1996
11	Benetton	1995		Lotus	1963		Ferrari	1998
10	Ferrari	2000		Lotus	1973		Ferrari	1999
	McLaren	1989		McLaren	1999		Lotus	1965
	Williams	1992		McLaren	2000		Lotus	1970
	Williams	1993		Tyrrell	1971		Matra	1969
9	Ferrari	2001		Williams	1991		McLaren	1976
	McLaren	1998		Williams	1994		McLaren	1985
	Williams	1986	**6**	Alfa Romeo	1950		McLaren	1990
	WIlliams	1987		Alfa Romeo	1951		Vanwall	1958
8	Benetton	1994		Cooper	1960		Williams	1980
	Lotus	1978		Ferrari	1975			
	McLaren	1991		Ferrari	1976			

MOST CONSECUTIVE WINS

9	Alberto Ascari	ITA	1952/53	Juan M Fangio	ARG	1953/54
6	M Schumacher	GER	2000/01	Damon Hill	GBR	1995/96
5	Jack Brabham	AUS	1960	Alain Prost	FRA	1993
	Jim Clark	GBR	1965	Jochen Rindt	AUT	1970
	Nigel Mansell	GBR	1992	M Schumacher	GER	1994
4	Jack Brabham	AUS	1966	Ayrton Senna	BRA	1988
	Jim Clark	GBR	1963	Ayrton Senna	BRA	1991

STARTS WITHOUT A WIN

208	Andrea de Cesaris	ITA	**109**	Philippe Alliot	FRA
158	Martin Bundle	GBR	**99**	Pedro Diniz	BRA
147	Derek Warwick	GBR	**97**	Chris Amon	NZL
135	Jean-Pierre Jarier	FRA	**95**	Ukyo Katayama	JAP
132	Eddie Cheever	USA	**94**	Mika Salo	FIN
119	Pierluigi Martini	ITA	**93**	Ivan Capelli	ITA

Victory Run: Michael Schumacher (19) jostles with Jean Alesi and Mika Hakkinen in the 1992 Belgian GP en route to his first Formula One win just a year after his debut

MOST FASTEST LAPS

DRIVERS

43	Michael Schumacher	GER		Ayrton Senna	BRA
41	Alain Prost	FRA	17	David Coulthard	GBR
30	Nigel Mansell	GBR	15	Clay Regazzoni	SUI
28	Jim Clark	GBR		Jackie Stewart	GBR
25	Mika Hakkinen	FIN	14	Jacky Ickx	BEL
	Niki Lauda	AUT	13	Alberto Ascari	ITA
23	Juan Manuel Fangio	ARG		Alan Jones	AUS
	Nelson Piquet	BRA		Riccardo Patrese	ITA
21	Gerhard Berger	AUT	12	René Arnoux	FRA
20	Stirling Moss	GBR		Jack Brabham	AUS
19	Damon Hill	GBR	11	John Surtees	GBR

CONSTRUCTORS

146	Ferrari	20	Tyrrell	12	Matra
119	Williams	18	Renault	11	Prost
107	McLaren	15	BRM	9	Mercedes
71	Lotus		Maserati	7	March
40	Brabham	14	Alfa Romeo	6	Vanwall
35	Benetton	13	Cooper		

MOST POLE POSITIONS

DRIVERS

65	Ayrton Senna	BRA	16	Stirling Moss	GBR
43	Michael Schumacher	GER	14	Alberto Ascari	ITA
33	Jim Clark	GBR		James Hunt	GBR
	Alain Prost	FRA		Ronnie Peterson	SWE
32	Nigel Mansell	GBR	13	Jack Brabham	AUS
29	Juan Manuel Fangio	ARG		Graham Hill	GBR
26	Mika Hakkinen	FIN		Jacky Ickx	BEL
24	Niki Lauda	AUT		Jacques Villeneuve	CDN
	Nelson Piquet	BRA	12	Gerhard Berger	AUT
20	Damon Hill	GBR		David Coulthard	GBR
18	Mario Andretti	USA	10	Jochen Rindt	AUT
	René Arnoux	FRA	8	Riccardo Patrese	ITA
17	Jackie Stewart	GBR		John Surtees	GBR

CONSTRUCTORS

148	Ferrari	14	Tyrrell	7	Vanwall
112	McLaren	12	Alfa Romeo	5	March
	Williams	11	BRM	4	Matra
107	Lotus		Cooper	3	Shadow
39	Brabham	10	Maserati	2	Jordan
31	Renault	9	Prost		Lancia
16	Benetton	8	Mercedes	1	Jaguar

IN ONE SEASON, DRIVERS

14	Nigel Mansell	GBR	1992		Ronnie Peterson	SWE	1973
13	Alain Prost	FRA	1993		Nelson Piquet	BRA	1984
	Ayrton Senna	BRA	1988		M Schumacher	GER	2000
	Ayrton Senna	BRA	1989	8	Mario Andretti	USA	1978
11	Mika Hakkinen	FIN	1999		James Hunt	GBR	1976
	M Schumacher	GER	2001		Nigel Mansell	GBR	1987
10	Ayrton Senna	BRA	1990		Ayrton Senna	BRA	1986
	J Villeneuve	CDN	1997		Ayrton Senna	BRA	1991
9	Mika Hakkinen	FIN	1998	7	Mario Andretti	USA	1977
	Damon Hill	GBR	1996		Jim Clark	GBR	1963
	Niki Lauda	AUT	1974		Damon Hill	GBR	1995
	Niki Lauda	AUT	1975		Ayrton Senna	BRA	1985

IN ONE SEASON, CONSTRUCTORS

15	McLaren	1988		Williams	1987		Ferrari	2000
	McLaren	1989		Williams	1995		Lotus	1973
	Williams	1992		Williams	1996		McLaren	1991
	Williams	1993	11	Ferrari	2001		Renault	1982
12	Lotus	1978		McLaren	1999	9	Brabham	1984
	McLaren	1990		Williams	1997		Ferrari	1975
	McLaren	1998	10	Ferrari	1974			

Mr Experience: Riccardo Patrese – here the winner of the enthralling 1982 Monaco GP – raced in more grands prix than anyone else: 256

Red Five: Nigel Mansell made this number famous when his Williams wore it in 1992, the year in which he finally won the world championship

MOST POINTS

This figure is gross tally, i.e. including scores that were later dropped

DRIVERS

801	Michael Schumacher	GER	310	Carlos Reutemann	ARG
798.5	Alain Prost	FRA	289	Graham Hill	GBR
614	Ayrton Senna	BRA	281	Emerson Fittipaldi	BRA
485.5	Nelson Piquet	BRA		Riccardo Patrese	ITA
482	Nigel Mansell	GBR	277.5	Juan Manuel Fangio	ARG
420.5	Niki Lauda	AUT	274	Jim Clark	GBR
420	Mika Hakkinen	FIN	261	Jack Brabham	AUS
385	Gerhard Berger	AUT	255	Jody Scheckter	ZA
360	Damon Hill	GBR	248	Denny Hulme	NZL
	Jackie Stewart	GBR	242	Jean Alesi	FRA
359	David Coulthard	GBR	228	Jacques Laffite	FRA

CONSTRUCTORS

2703.5	Ferrari	439	BRM	155	Matra
2582.5	McLaren	424	Prost	112	Sauber
2111.5	Williams	333	Cooper	79	Wolf
1352	Lotus	312	Renault	67.5	Shadow
877.5	Benetton	250	Jordan	60	Jaguar
854	Brabham	171.5	March	57	Vanwall
617	Tyrrell	165	Arrows	54	Surtees

MOST TITLES

DRIVERS

5	Juan Manuel Fangio	ARG	1	Mario Andretti	USA
4	Alain Prost	FRA		Giuseppe Farina	ITA
	Michael Schumacher	GER		Mike Hawthorn	GBR
3	Jack Brabham	AUS		Damon Hill	GBR
	Niki Lauda	AUT		Phil Hill	USA
	Nelson Piquet	BRA		Denny Hulme	NZL
	Ayrton Senna	BRA		James Hunt	GBR
	Jackie Stewart	GBR		Alan Jones	AUS
2	Alberto Ascari	ITA		Nigel Mansell	GBR
	Jim Clark	GBR		Jochen Rindt	AUT
	Emerson Fittipaldi	BRA		Keke Rosberg	FIN
	Mika Hakkinen	FIN		Jody Scheckter	RSA
	Graham Hill	GBR		John Surtees	GBR
				Jacques Villeneuve	CDN

CONSTRUCTORS

11	Ferrari	2	Brabham		Matra
9	Williams		Cooper		Tyrrell
8	McLaren	1	Benetton		Vanwall
7	Lotus		BRM		

THE VENUES 2002

Anyone who says that one circuit is like another has either never watched ITV's television coverage or even ventured trackside, for there's a wealth of variety around the globe.

Had they done so, then they would never mistake Spa-Francorchamps for Hockenheim or Silverstone. Indeed, one of the greatest draws to Formula One is the sheer variety, not just from the 17 different circuits, but also from the very different countries around the globe in which the World Championship rounds are held. Some love Monaco for the glitz and glamour of the yachts and the casino, others rate Suzuka as the best for the precision that drivers need to put together a fast lap. But that's the beauty of the World Championship, as no two circuits are the same and variety is definitely the spice of life.

AUSTRALIAN GP ROUND 1

Date 3 March 2002 **Circuit Name** Albert Park

Laps 58 **Circuit Length** 3.295 miles / 5.302 km
Lap record Michael Schumacher (Ferrari), 1m 28.214s, 134.468mph / 216.36kph, 2001
Website www.grandprix.com.au
Location Just south of the centre of Melbourne
Description A flat and twisting circuit around a lake, with no long straights but a highish average lap speed of 132mph.
Best Viewing Turn 1, Turn 3 and Turn 12

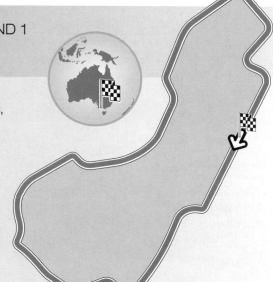

Previous Winners

1997
David Coulthard
McLaren

1998
Mika Hakkinen
McLaren

1999
Eddie Irvine
Ferrari

2000
Michael Schumacher
Ferrari

2001
Michael Schumacher
Ferrari

Previous Winners

1999
Eddie Irvine
Ferrari

2000
Michael Schumacher
Ferrari

2001
Michael Schumacher
Ferrari

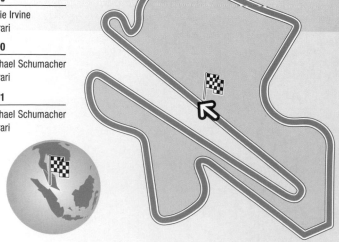

MALAYSIAN GP ROUND 2

Date 17 March 2002 **Circuit Name** Sepang

Laps 56 **Circuit Length** 3.444 miles / 5.542km
Lap record Mika Hakkinen (McLaren), 1m 38.543s, 125.817mph / 202.474kph, 2000
Website www.malaysiangp.com.my
Location 30km south of Kuala Lumpur
Description Circuit designer Hermann Tilke's best new track, offering unusually long straights mixed with flowing and bends over a gently undulating course. The final hairpin is excellent for overtaking.
Best Viewing Turn 1, Turn 4 and Turn 15

BRAZILIAN GP ROUND 3

Date 31 March 2002 **Circuit Name** Interlagos

Laps 71 **Circuit Length** 2.667 miles / 4.292km
Lap record Michael Schumacher (Ferrari), 1m 14.755s,
128.436mph / 206.687kph, 2000
Website www.ainterlagos.com
Location 16km south of central São Paulo
Description An increasingly decrepit circuit that sits wonderfully
in an amphitheatre, affording great views from the grandstands
at the top of the hill. The plunging first corner is a treat.
Drivers have to work for their living over the many bumps,
especially as it can be very hot.
Best Viewing Curva 1, Descida do Lago and Arquibancadas

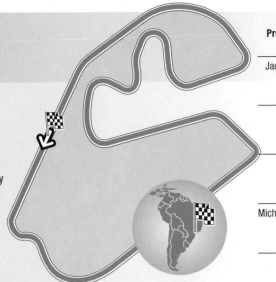

Previous Winners
1997
Jacques Villeneuve
Williams
1998
Mika Hakkinen
McLaren
1999
Mika Hakkinen
McLaren
2000
Michael Schumacher
Ferrari
2001
David Coulthard
McLaren

Previous Winners
1997
Heinz-Harald Frentzen
Williams
1998
David Coulthard
McLaren
1999
Michael Schumacher
Ferrari
2000
Michael Schumacher
Ferrari
2001
Ralf Schumacher
Williams

SAN MARINO GP ROUND 4

Date 14 April 2002 **Circuit Name** Imola

Laps 62 **Circuit Length** 3.064 miles / 4.930km
Lap record Ralf Schumacher (Williams), 1m 25.524s,
128.974mph / 207.554kph, 2001
Website www.autodromoimola.com
Location North-eastern suburbs of Imola,
33km south-east of Bologna
Description A wonderful, undulating circuit in a parkland setting,
with its former high-speed blasts along the bottom of the valley
now interrupted by chicanes. But the down-then-up Acque Minerali
remains a wonderful place from which to watch in qualifying.
Best Viewing Tosa, Rivazza and Variante Bassa

REPUBBLICA DI SAN MARINO

SPANISH GP ROUND 5

Date 28 April 2002 **Circuit Name** Circuit de Catalunya

Laps 65 **Circuit Length** 2.949 miles / 4.727km
Lap record Michael Schumacher (Ferrari), 1m 21.151s,
130.823mph / 210.529kph, 2001
Website www.circuitcat.com
Location At Montmelo, 20km north of Barcelona
Description Blessed with one of the longest straights in F1 leading
into a tight first corner, there should be lots of overtaking here.
But, because the corner onto the straight (called New Holland)
is a flat-out one, this doesn't happen as much as it ought to.
Campsa corner at the crest of a hill can be spectacular.
Best Viewing Elf, La Caixa and New Holland

Previous Winners
1997
Jacques Villeneuve
Williams
1998
Mika Hakkinen
McLaren
1999
Mika Hakkinen
McLaren
2000
Mika Hakkinen
McLaren
2001
Michael Schumacher
Ferrari

Previous Winners

1997

Jacques Villeneuve
Williams

1998

Mika Hakkinen
McLaren

1999

Eddie Irvine
Ferrari

2000

Mika Hakkinen
McLaren

2001

David Coulthard
McLaren

AUSTRIAN GP ROUND 6

Date 12 May 2002 **Circuit Name** A1-Ring

Laps 71 **Circuit Length** 2.685 miles / 4.326km
Lap record David Coulthard (McLaren), 1m 10.843s,
136.443mph / 219.573kph, 2001
Website www.a1ring.at
Location 70km north-west of Graz and 200km south-east of Salzburg
Description One of the shortest tracks on the calendar,
this is effectively a truncated version of the Osterreichring that hosted
the Austrian GP until 1987. Situated on a mountainside, this track offers
the longest climb in F1 from the startline to Remus Kurve which, along with
Castrol Kurve, also offers a couple of F1's best overtaking places.
Best Viewing Castrol Kurve, Remus Kurve and Gösser Kurve

MONACO GP ROUND 7

Date 26 May 2002 **Circuit Name** Monte Carlo

Laps 78 **Circuit Length** 2.092 miles / 3.367km
Lap record David Coulthard (McLaren), 1m 19.424s,
94.823mph / 152.595kph, 2001
Website www.acm.mc
Location Monte Carlo, Monaco
Description An anachronism as it wends its way uphill and
down between the houses of the Principality. The only fast stretch
is through the tunnel, so maximum downforce is the order of the
day. The track is too narrow for overtaking, and lined with barriers
over its entire length, but many still try into Ste Dévote.
Best Viewing Ste Dévote, Nouvelle Chicane and Piscine

Previous Winners
1997

Michael Schumacher
Ferrari

1998

Mika Hakkinen
McLaren

1999

Michael Schumacher
Ferrari

2000

David Coulthard
McLaren

2001

Michael Schumacher
Ferrari

Previous Winners
1997

Michael Schumacher
Ferrari

1998

Michael Schumacher
Ferrari

1999

Mika Hakkinen
McLaren

2000

Michael Schumacher
Ferrari

2001

Ralf Schumacher
Williams

CANADIAN GP ROUND 8
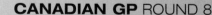

Date 9 June 2002 **Circuit Name** Circuit Gilles-Villeneuve

Laps 69 **Circuit Length** 2.747 miles / 4.421km
Lap record Ralf Schumacher (Williams), 1m 17.205s,
128.090mph / 206.132kph, 2001
Website www.grandprix.ca
Location On Île de Notre Dame in Montreal
Description Flat by nature and flat-out too,
with long straights between two hairpins linked by
fast esses and a sharp chicane onto the start/finish straight. A concrete
wall-lined car-breaker of a circuit that hammers brakes and transmissions.
Best Viewing Coin Senna, Virage du Casino and Turn 6

EUROPEAN GP ROUND 9

Date 23 June 2002 **Circuit Name** Nürburgring

Laps 67 **Circuit Length** 2.831 miles / 4.556km
Lap record Juan Pablo Montoya (Williams), 1m 18.354,
130.071mph / 209.320kph, 2001
Website www.nuerburgring.de
Location 60km north of Koblenz, 90km south-west of Cologne
Description Finally acknowledged as being a worthwhile circuit after
years of being compared to the mighty Nordschleife, on part of which
it was built. Another mixed and undulating circuit that compromises
chassis set-up. The run to the first corner provides overtaking possibilities.
The weather can change quickly as it's in the Eifel mountains.
Best Viewing Castrol-S, Veedol Schikane and Coca-Cola Kurve

Previous Winners
1997
Jacques Villeneuve
Williams
1998
Mika Hakkinen
McLaren
1999
Johnny Herbert
Stewart
2000
Michael Schumacher
Ferrari
2001
Michael Schumacher
Ferrari

Previous Winners
1997
Jacques Villeneuve
Williams
1998
Michael Schumacher
Ferrari
1999
David Coulthard
McLaren
2000
David Coulthard
McLaren
2001
Mika Hakkinen
McLaren

BRITISH GP ROUND 10

Date 7 July 2002 **Circuit Name** Silverstone

Laps 60 **Circuit Length** 3.194 miles / 5.140km
Lap record Mika Hakkinen (McLaren), 1m 23.405s,
137.862mph / 221.857kph, 2001
Website www.silverstone-circuit.co.uk
Location 25km south-west of Northampton and
90km north-west of London
Description Built on a former airfield, this circuit seems to have a
modified layout every year, but has somewhat lost its flat-out nature of old.
Copse and the Becketts sweepers are very impressive. A radically new layout is
due for 2003 that will see the pitlane and paddock move to between Club and Abbey.
Best Viewing Copse, Becketts and Stowe

FRENCH GP ROUND 11

Date 21 July 2002 **Circuit Name** Magny-Cours

Laps 72 **Circuit Length** 2.641 miles / 4.250km
Lap record David Coulthard (McLaren), 1m 16.088s,
124.955mph / 201.087kph, 2001
Website www.magny-cours.com
Location 10km south of Nevers, 250km south of Paris
Description This super-smooth track is a technical one with every
sort of corner from low-speed hairpins to fast chicanes and
medium-speed corners. Heinz-Harald Frentzen described it thus:
"One of the most exciting circuits as the corners are challenging,
especially the first left-right combination. It flows very well."
Best Viewing Estoril, Adelaide and Château d'Eau

Previous Winners
1997
Michael Schumacher
Ferrari
1998
Michael Schumacher
Ferrari
1999
Heinz-Harald Frentzen
Jordan
2000
David Coulthard
McLaren
2001
Michael Schumacher
Ferrari

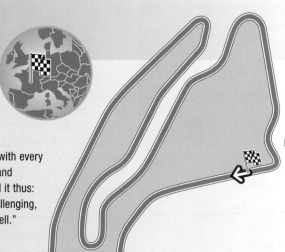

GERMAN GP ROUND 12

Date 28 July 2002 **Circuit Name** Hockenheim

Laps 69 **Circuit Length** 2.780 miles / 4.470 km
Lap record Juan Pablo Montoya (Williams), 1m 41.808s,
149.929mph / 241.277kph, 2001
Website www.hockenheimring.de
Location 25km south of Heidelberg, 90km south of Frankfurt
Description Changes are afoot for 2002 when the track will
be truncated. One amazing feature of the outgoing layout
is that up to 70 percent of the lap is spent with the cars at
full throttle. Crowd noise in the stadium section is awesome.
Best Viewing Nordkurve, Agipkurve and Sachskurve

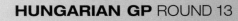

Previous Winners
1997
Gerhard Berger
Benetton
1998
Mika Hakkinen
McLaren
1999
Eddie Irvine
Ferrari
2000
Rubens Barrichello
Ferrari
2001
Ralf Schumacher
Williams

Previous Winners
1997
Jacques Villeneuve
Williams
1998
Michael Schumacher
Ferrari
1999
Mika Hakkinen
McLaren
2000
Mika Hakkinen
McLaren
2001
Michael Schumacher
Ferrari

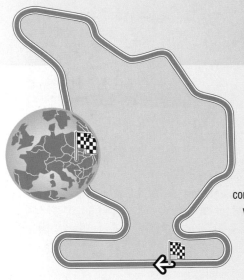

HUNGARIAN GP ROUND 13

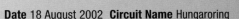

Date 18 August 2002 **Circuit Name** Hungaroring

Laps 77 **Circuit Length** 2.469 miles / 3.973km
Lap record Mika Hakkinen (McLaren), 1m 16.723s,
115.851mph / 186.435kph, 2001
Website www.hungaroring.hu
Location 20km north-east of Budapest
Description A technical circuit that keeps the drivers more
busy rather than as challenged as at some circuits since its
corners tend to be low-speed. Its location in a valley offers excellent
viewing from the start/finish straight and also on the far side from
Turn 5 to Turn 10. The rush to the dipping first corner is
always exciting. The weather tends to be very hot.
Best Viewing Turn 1, Turn 6 and Turn 13

BELGIAN GP ROUND 14

Date 1 September 2002 **Circuit Name** Spa-Francorchamps

Laps 44 **Circuit Length** 4.329 miles / 6.968km
Lap record Michael Schumacher (Ferrari), 1m 49.758s,
141.989mph / 228.498kph, 2001
Website www.spa-francorchamps.be
Location 50km south-east of Liège
Description The greatest circuit on the calendar, with several
world-class corners around its lengthy, high-speed lap.
Eau Rouge is the ultimate test of mind over matter, the
double-apex, off-camber Pouhon requires precision, while
Blanchimont proved last year that it can bite. The weather
is usually fickle in the Ardennes, though, so take an umbrella.
Best Viewing Eau Rouge, Les Combes and the Bus Stop

Previous Winners
1997
Michael Schumacher
Ferrari
1998
Damon Hill
Jordan
1999
David Coulthard
McLaren
2000
Mika Hakkinen
McLaren
2001
Michael Schumacher
Ferrari

Previous Winners

1997

David Coulthard
McLaren

1998

Michael Schumacher
Ferrari

1999

Heinz-Harald Frentzen
Jordan

2000

Michael Schumacher
Ferrari

2001

Juan Pablo Montoya
Williams

ITALIAN GP ROUND 15

Date 15 September 2002 **Circuit Name** Monza

Laps 53 **Circuit Length** 3.600 miles / 5.793km
Lap record Ralf Schumacher (Williams), 1m 25.073s,
152.340mph / 245.156kph, 2001
Website www.monzanet.it
Location On the northern outskirts of Monza, 16km north-west of Milan
Description A circuit with a real history, Monza's now-unused banked section is a poignant reminder of days gone by. Its first and second chicanes remain unloved, breaking the original flat-out flow, though the second one should be modified for 2002. David Coulthard reckons that if the first chicane is to be kept, it should be re-profiled so that it's like the last chicane at Imola. The Ferrari-supporting *tifosi* are the most partisan fans in the world.
Best Viewing Rettifilo Tribune, Variante Ascari and Curva Parabolica

---

 # UNITED STATES GP ROUND 16

Date 29 September 2002 **Circuit Name** Indianapolis Motor Speedway

Laps 73 **Circuit Length** 2.606 miles / 4.195km
Lap record Juan Pablo Montoya (Williams-BMW), 1m 14.448s,
125.967mph / 202.715kph, 2001
Website www.my.brickyard.com
Location In the western suburbs of Indianapolis, Indiana
Description A section of the banking between Turns 1 and 2 of the oval leads in reverse direction onto the main straight before ducking into a twisting infield section. Jacques Villeneuve said it had "no corner where your heartbeat goes up", but that it was a "fun track" as you have to work hard on the infield to get close to the car ahead for an attack down the long straight.
Best Viewing Turn 1, Turn 8 and Turn 13

Previous Winners
2000

Michael Schumacher
Ferrari

2001

Mika Hakkinen
McLaren

Previous Winners

1997

Michael Schumacher
Ferrari

1998

Mika Hakkinen
McLaren

1999

Mika Hakkinen
McLaren

2000

Michael Schumacher
Ferrari

2001

Michael Schumacher
Ferrari

JAPANESE GP ROUND 17

Date 13 October 2002 **Circuit Name** Suzuka

Laps 53 **Circuit Length** 3.641 miles / 5.859km
Lap record Ralf Schumacher (Williams), 1m 36.944s,
135.319mph / 217.728kph, 2001
Website www.SuzukaCircuit.co.jp
Location 50km south-west of Nagoya, 150km east of Osaka
Description Second only to Spa-Francorchamps in terms of a challenge to the drivers, this circuit situated amid an amusement park has some real tests, such as the uphill esses, the long Spoon Curve and the mighty, flat-out 130R. The grandstands around much of its twisting perimeter are packed dawn to dusk with knowledgeable fans.
Best Viewing First Curve, Hairpin and Casio Triangle

2002 FIA FORMULA ONE

	Driver	Car	March 3 **AUSTRALIAN GP**	March 17 **MALAYSIAN GP**	March 31 **BRAZILIAN GP**	April 14 **SAN MARINO GP**	April 28 **SPANISH GP**	May 12 **AUSTRIAN GP**	May 26 **MONACO GP**
1	MICHAEL SCHUMACHER	Ferrari							
2	RUBENS BARRICHELLO	Ferrari							
3	DAVID COULTHARD	McLaren							
4	KIMI RÄIKKÖNEN	McLaren							
5	RALF SCHUMACHER	Williams							
6	JUAN PABLO MONTOYA	Williams							
7	NICK HEIDFELD	Sauber							
8	FELIPE MASSA	Sauber							
9	GIANCARLO FISICHELLA	Jordan							
10	TAKUMA SATO	Jordan							
11	JACQUES VILLENEUVE	BAR							
12	OLIVIER PANIS	BAR							
14	JARNO TRULLI	Renault							
15	JENSON BUTTON	Renault							
16	EDDIE IRVINE	Jaguar							
17	PEDRO DE LA ROSA	Jaguar							
18	JOS VERSTAPPEN?	Prost							
19	TBA	Prost							
20	HEINZ-HARALD FRENTZEN?	Arrows							
21	ENRIQUE BERNOLDI	Arrows							
22	ALEX YOONG	Minardi							
23	TBA	Minardi							
24	MIKA SALO	Toyota							
25	ALLAN MCNISH	Toyota							

WORLD CHAMPIONSHIP

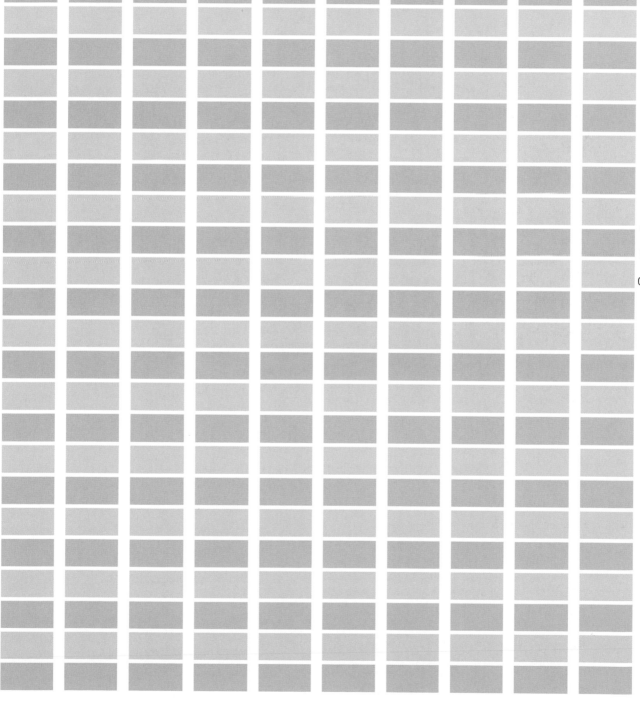

CANADIAN GP	June 23 EUROPEAN GP	July 7 BRITISH GP	July 21 FRENCH GP	July 28 GERMAN GP	August 18 HUNGARIAN GP	September 1 BELGIAN GP	September 15 ITALIAN GP	September 29 UNITED STATES GP	October 13 JAPANESE GP	Points Total

127

2002 FIA
FORMULA ONE
WORLD
CHAMPIONSHIP

Scoring system: 10, 6, 4, 3, 2, 1 for the first six finishers

Respected Rivals: Michael Schumacher wishes Mika Hakkinen well for his one-year sabbatical after they'd finished the Japanese GP

The publishers would like to thank the following sources for their kind permission to reproduce the pictures in this book:

Allsport UK Ltd 58, Bryn Lennon 86, Clive Mason 7, 20, 30, 36, 41, 52, 96, 97, 101, 104, 109, Pascal Rondeau 84, 117, Mark Thompson 2, 39, 100, 105, 110, 123, 125

Empics 13/ Mike Egerton 66, John Marsh 6, 35, 36, 85, Steve Mitchell 3, 4l, 5r, 10, 11,12, 14,15, 16, 21, 23, 24, 25, 26, 30, 33, 38, 43, 45, 46, 47, 48, 50, 64, 65, 70-1b, 71tl, 76, 78, 79, 80, 81, 82, 83, 87, 92, 108b, 111br, 111tl, 121, 122, 128, Neal Simpson 17, 32, 34, 44, Phil Walter 27

LAT Photographic 5l, 8-9, 18, 19, 22, 28, 29, 40, 42, 54, 57, 59, 68-9, 70tl, 70tr, 71tr, 72, 73, 74, 75, 77, 90, 91, 93, 94, 95, 98, 99, 102, 108tr, 112, 114, 118-9, 124, Martyn Elford 4r

Sutton Motorsport Images 89, 103, 113, 115, 116, Pan Images 31, Bearne 88

Every effort has been made to acknowledge correctly and contact the source and/or copyright holder of each picture, and Carlton Books Limited apologises for any unintentional errors or omissions which will be corrected in future editions of this book.